BE

~ *that* ~

ENGINEER:

INSPIRATION

AND

INSIGHT

from

ACCOMPLISHED

women

ENGINEERS

Publisher:
Society of Women Engineers
203 N La Salle Street, Suite 1675
Chicago, IL 60601
www.swe.org

Design and Content Management by the David James Group

Contributors: Decie Autin, Priya Bajoria, Liz Buzzard, Marietta Cleveland, Lisa Engel, Diane Foley, Elizabeth Fuhrman, Gayle Gibson, Lynda Grindstaff, Rachel Heidenreich, Afsaneh Sunnie House, Jennifer Howland, Stacy Johnson, Dr. Ruth Jones, Andrea Karalus, Mariana Karam, Ellen Kerr, Susan Lewis, Nan Mattai, Maryann McNally, Judy Moses, Marla Peterson, Emily Plunkett, Sharon Rozzi, Jennifer Rumsey, Vicky Saye, Margaret Simone, Patricia Solliday, Lauren Streb, Jean Bennington Sweeney, Melissa Tata, Karen Tokashiki, Shirley Yap

ISBN-13: 978-0692238905
ISBN-10: 0692238905

First Edition

Printed in the United States of America by CreateSpace,
An Amazon.com Company

Contents

Foreward

In early 2014 a team of us at the headquarters of the Society of
Women Engineers (SWE) had an idea: what if we asked the amazing
women leaders of our Corporate Partnership Council (CPC) for their
stories and words of inspiration? After all, these are women who chose
to enter engineering and technology, have worked hard, accomplished
much and have risen to leadership positions in their organizations.
They are also women who have by and large found creative ways to
balance their careers and personal lives. Who better to inspire fellow
and future women in engineering and technology?

So, we asked for their contributions and received numerous
submissions. From the heartfelt to the practical, we were excited
to read their entries and are excited to share them with you in this
wonderful book.

The power of inspiration, mentorship, support and encouraging words
from our community should not be underestimated. They matter, as
this testimonial I received clearly demonstrates:

I wanted to share my good news with you. I have been promoted.
I am so thrilled. This is an absolute dream job for me. I feel like I
want to do a SWE testimonial. I truly would not be here without the
wonderful support and mentoring I have gotten from the amazing
women at SWE. Mary P. and Florence H., in particular have
invested their time and vast knowledge in mentoring me, and their

help and perspective have been invaluable. Thank you for leading an organization with such amazing executives! And thank you personally for your friendship and support.
Very warmest regards,

Rachel Hutter, PE

I encourage you to read this book, absorb our contributors' words and continue to be that engineer who makes a difference, both personally and professionally.

Karen Horting, MBA, CAE
Executive Director & CEO
Society of Women Engineers

CHAPTER
~ 1 ~

BEING A
LEADER
in a

MALE-DOMINATED
WORK PLACE

"There are things in a male-dominated workplace that may seem like a hindrance. However, focusing on the hindrances does not get you ahead. By turning your focus to the opportunities, you can embrace the differences **"**

Decie Autin

Project Executive, ExxonMobil

I discovered early in my career that the key to being an effective female leader in a male-dominated work place is approaching individuals and situations in a non-aggressive manner and from the perspective of helping. Once you demonstrate that you are committed to doing the right thing and can be effective and helpful, the majority of folks will follow you. When I was a young engineer working offshore as the second woman ever to work there, I found folks testing my commitment with verbal taunts and some pranks meant to make me think twice about staying. I spoke to several folks, and identified a project they had been trying to get done for over five years, but had not been able to justify. I worked with them to design the change, which involved consolidating operations from three platforms onto one platform. I took the proposal to management and got it approved. Working together, we executed the project in six months. I have been fast friends with all those team members ever since. I have used this strategy as I progressed into management and have found it works with engineers and managers, as well as with offshore wage earners.

Marietta Cleveland

Quality Center Manager, Chrysler Group LLC

Early on in my career, I learned not to take offense so easily. Oftentimes, in a male-dominated environment, some of the comments and/or language can be a bit distasteful. You gain their trust when you allow guys to be themselves around you. Now, there is a line that should not be crossed, and most guys do not intend to show disrespect and cross the line of what is known to be out of bounds.

Lisa Engel

Vice President New Product Development & Marketing, Emerson

We've all been there. A twenty-something recent graduate taking our first job, and worried that more seasoned colleagues will judge us on Day One. When I was still a twenty-something working for my third employer, I was responsible for the design and development of an electromechanical device. One day, I confidently entered the lab to discuss a testing protocol on a new design. The technician, who could've been my father, was a twenty-year veteran. He looked me in the eye, and proclaimed, "I've had to put up with so many of you young, know-it-all-engineers, but now a girl?" I was taken aback and nearly speechless (which isn't common for me). He drew a line in the sand. I had to earn his respect to cross it. So, I burned the midnight oil, did the dirty work, asked him for input, and never gave up till the problem was solved. We had many successful years together. At his retirement, he told me he enjoyed working together, and said, "You're pretty smart, even though you're a girl." In the end, he allowed me to cross his line, and our professional relationship transcended generations and stereotypes. Till this day, we stay in touch.

Elizabeth Fuhrman

Associate Manager, Advanced Quality, Stryker

There are things in a male-dominated workplace that may seem like a hindrance; for example, a lack of sports knowledge, a different approach to raises and promotions, or to childcare and rearing. However, focusing on the hindrances does not get you ahead. By turning your focus to the opportunities, you can embrace the differences and add some estrogen to the workplace for your benefit. First, be yourself because people will appreciate a real person and not an imposter. Secondly, demonstrate how you add value and deliver on results. Third, let's look at some womanly features to set you apart. Personally, I'm known for my baking. Sometimes, the classification gets old, and there is a slight cost and time associated with it. However, I have built relationships with people and opportunities for favors with my tasty treats. I have also used this enjoyable hobby to encourage meeting attendance when a topic may be dry or not a favorite. I also personalize thank you gifts with home-baked goods. Other womanly traits I have used to my advantage include my planning ability for team outings, creating a more welcoming environment with warmth and friendliness, and displaying my warm, caring side in all situations.

Lynda Grindstaff

Director of Innovation Solutions, Intel Security Group,
Intel Corporation

Current and future generations can make a change in the professional landscape of engineers by truly understanding why it is beneficial to have diverse teams. Not just diverse in terms of men and women, but also diverse in terms of backgrounds, colleges attended, and ethnicity, just to name a few. Studies have shown that diverse teams outperform groups of like-minded individuals, and it's this not many people are aware of, which is why education is also needed. This change also requires educating all engineers about the needs of these diverse groups so they don't create biases based upon stereotypes, but instead are industry influencers and supporters of people who don't look like themselves or come from a similar background. When we have an environment where people understand the needs of others and support each other, then we will start to see leaders at all levels from all different ways of life.

Rachel Heidenreich

Vice President of Quality & Continuous Improvement,
Rockwell Automation

I became a leader early in my working career. After four years of engineering experience and two years of graduate school, I became a supervisor in tool engineering. At age 27, I led a team of 10 that exceeded me in age by 10 to 30 years, and were all male. Although they worked for me, I quickly became a "leader through influence" as I did not have tooling expertise or managerial experience to rely on. Despite my lack of confidence, I found that I could influence this team to follow my lead. As an example, early on, they arrived late to staff meetings and hesitated to speak up. I instituted a rule that the last person to the meeting was responsible for the "joke of the day." Since most of them preferred not to tell jokes, they quickly became very punctual, while we started each meeting with a laugh. Along with learning to influence, I worked very hard and listened to them closely. Over time, it was a great experience in developing key skills in leading people. The fundamentals of influencing, working hard, and listening supported additional increases in responsibilities throughout my career.

Afsaneh Sunnie House

Vice President, Southwest Coast Sub Region Manager,
URS Corporation

Passion, perseverance, and poise are words that describe many successful women leaders, including me. These attributes have been instilled in me by supportive and reassuring parents who taught me to be strong despite any gender inequalities imposed by my society. This was quite progressive for my parents who raised four daughters in Iran in the 1960s. As their eldest daughter, I was constantly reminded that women can achieve great feats, and that the sky was the limit for me. My advancement to leadership positions within the engineering community stems from this belief. My ambition and confidence in my abilities have always been my guiding light in pursuing new opportunities and stepping up for new challenges. Throughout my career, I have only once come across a male colleague who felt that women should be "barefoot and pregnant in the kitchen" (1984). Funny thing was he told me this while I was pregnant, unbeknownst to him. He soon came to respect my work and accepted me as a valuable member of the team.

Jennifer Howland

Executive, Pathways for Experienced Technical Women,
IBM CHQ, IBM

Early in my career, I was invited to participate in a women's roundtable. At the roundtable, a woman engineer spoke up about her concern of not being seen as "one of the guys." For example, she was offended because she was never included when the men went to lunch. She mentioned she would always eat with some women friends from another area. I remember not being able to relate to her concern. Being the only women engineer in my department, I didn't have anyone else with whom to go to lunch besides some of the men, so they included me. I became comfortable in this environment, which served me well throughout my career. There are many hurdles women have to jump over to advance, but sometimes we don't make it easy on ourselves. The woman was unknowingly isolating herself by always eating lunch with her friends, instead of trying to get to know some of her male peers in a different environment. Had she not spent every lunch break with her friends, there would have been a better chance of having that informal inclusion happen. Don't isolate yourself, keep a sense of humor, and above all, work hard.

Dr. Ruth Jones

Mishap Investigation Specialist, NASA Safety Center

Being a woman in a male-dominated field can be a bit intimidating, but the key to surviving is knowing your subject matter, and not being afraid to ask for help and/or say you don't know. Throughout my work career, I have been the only female in my work organization. I can remember clearly at my first team meeting, there was a question on the floor, and one of my co-workers said, "Ask Dr. Ruth. She has a PhD." I thought to myself, "If I had been a male with a PhD, then I would not have been put on the spot like that." That incident made me a true leader because it taught me to not be afraid to say I don't know even with a PhD, and it encouraged me to know my subject matter. I would encourage all future engineers, especially female engineers of the future, to get all the education they can because education is the key to success. "Education is like Coca Cola—it is the real thing. Education is like General Electric—it will light your path. Education is like Scotch Tape—you can't see it, but you know it's there, and education is like American Express—you can NEVER leave home without it." And even with the highest degree, you will still not know everything, and it is OK!

Mariana Karam

Business Manager-Front End Equipment, Global Crop Harvesting
Platform, Deere & Company

I never stop feeling like a pioneer. That feeling started for me at the
University of Notre Dame in 1981, where the ratio was 4:1, men to
women. As a mechanical engineering major, most of my classes had
only one or two women. To top it off, I was an ROTC student – Marine
Corps option! In 1985, I became the first female commissioned
Marine Corps officer graduate at Notre Dame. Serving as a woman
officer in the Marine Corps at a time when there were fewer than
1,000 of them was a great adventure, to say the least! It was wonderful
to join other women engineers at John Deere in 1991. We were truly
pioneers for the company. I felt so fortunate to be among the first to
work in Asia (Japan, China, India), as a manager in emerging Brazil,
and as one of our company's first women factory managers in Europe.
These experiences have now become the norm, not the exception.
We've not only lived the adventure of pioneers, but we've also left a
legacy for the next generation. Of course, I won't be waiting for new
opportunities to come my way. I'll be seeking them out!

Ellen Kerr

Vice President, Operations Engineering Manager, FM Global

To be honest, being a woman in a male-dominated work place has never been a factor. What I mean is that it isn't anything I have ever focused or dwelled on. The emphasis really should be on how each person can contribute to the success of an organization regardless of its makeup. One should understand how success is defined for each role they are in and concentrate on that. Another key is the role of advocates. These are people one works with at all levels within the organization who lobby on your behalf. They promote your abilities to others, such as when a project needs volunteers, a task force is being established, or there is a new opening. Advocates help your voice get heard and can be critical to your success.

Susan Lewis

Vice President, Dow AgroSciences Operations,
The Dow Chemical Company

Throughout academia and for most of my career, I never really thought about being in a male-dominated workforce. Throughout engineering school, results were key, not your gender. I focused on that same philosophy in the workplace. Deliver the results, and that would earn respect and enable success. It's true that results are important, but it's also about HOW you achieve those results, especially if you aspire to be a leader. Sometimes it's not easy when you are working with many personalities, differing opinions, and work styles. Collaboration and inclusion are important to bring together teams or workgroups to deliver those desired team results. It's not just about the individual – male or female. My advice is to put aside your own bias or thoughts about what it means to be in a male-dominated work place. When you focus on collaboration and achievement for the greater whole, barriers break down and you pave the way for your success as well as your team's success.

Judy Moses

General Manager Asset Development,
MidContinent Business Unit, Chevron

My advice on being a leader in a male-dominated workplace: You don't have to try to fit in completely. Just be yourself and focus primarily on the job. For example, if your colleagues have a lot of interest in sports, but you don't, it's not necessary to pretend interest. Some of the best advice I received earlier in my career is that you have work colleagues at work and make close friends separately. I believe this is good advice for any leader because of all the inherent conflicts in managing employees who are close friends, but it particularly applies to women leading a group of mostly men. Things have changed a lot since I started in the industry – there are far more women in the engineering workforce today, and I think this is a more subtle issue than it was in earlier years. However, women still must focus on professionalism in order to be seen as a strong and effective leaders of both male and female peers. So my advice is to feel free to talk a little about family and personal topics, but strike a strong balance toward focusing primarily on the work.

Emily Plunkett

Sr. Structural Engineer 3A, L-3 Communications

Confidence. It may not be uncommon for new female engineers to enter the workplace lacking self-confidence, when compared with their male counterparts. If you do not believe in yourself, it will be very difficult for others to believe in you. It is important to recognize that you are an educated engineer who deserves the position you have earned. Take credit for your successes and do not worry too much about making mistakes. We are all human and we make mistakes; the trick is to make sure you learn from your mistakes. Engineering is a difficult discipline with a steep learning curve. By graduating with an engineering degree, you have proven that you are capable of handling rigorous and challenging tasks. Do not be afraid to step outside of your comfort zone by taking on more responsibility and constantly learning new tools and skills. As a lead engineer, you will sometimes feel under prepared, overwhelmed and overextended. Remember that these are opportunities to learn and grow. Challenges are opportunities to prove to yourself, your coworkers and your manager that you are capable of handling difficult assignments.

Sharon Rozzi

Senior Director Operations, Medtronic

The first organization I joined after school was very male-dominated and isolating. People were closed off. I had difficulty finding a mentor within the department to ease my transition. Not surprisingly, the business was not performing well. In less than two years, I was looking for a move. Thanks to a mentor from another department, I had the good fortune of an offer from another business in that company. I could see from the start that new organization was a supportive environment for women. Women made up about 30% of the technical workforce. That organization was relentlessly customer focused. That focus drove collaboration and a culture where people put gender and ethic differences aside. The senior most technical person was a woman, and she became my manager, mentor, and sponsor. Over the years, she created many stretch opportunities for me to develop and advance. My advice to women in engineering is twofold. First, seek out a supportive environment. Second, be authentic. Rather than adopt a male leadership style, be true to your natural style. I firmly believe that a female leadership style can be a refreshing change, and refreshing can get you noticed and help you influence.

Margaret Simone

Senior Project Manager, Turner Construction Company

When I first thought of studying engineering, it had less to do with a career and more to do with the things I was interested in learning. I noticed the disproportionate ratio of males to females in my classes and professors, but it wasn't until I started down the path of a career in construction that the differences became so dramatic. From the construction managers to the design professionals to the labor force, my interaction was almost entirely with males. I had no construction experience, and was not particularly welcome on the jobsite. I certainly could not tell men with decades of experience how to do their job, so I began carving out my place by establishing my usefulness as an information getter and provider. I soon realized that information was a powerful tool, and knowledge creates the perfect platform for influence. Being a reliable source of answers had no gender, and became a value to those trying to stay on schedule. I fought the pressure to conform to the male approach to leadership, and found it more important to define that for myself and find my own unique way to make an impact on my projects.

Patricia Solliday

Senior R&D Engineer, Boston Scientific

Leading in a traditional male-dominated field requires you to be intentional about building specific gender relationships. It is important to have a well-rounded network of both genders at diverse, cross-functional levels to help stay connected. Relationships are equally as important as being a technically competent high contributor. When preparing for important meetings, I find it valuable to thoroughly prepare material and anticipate questions and concerns. I also review the invite list ahead of time to inventory the team players and their influential power. This allows me to actively participate and contribute at a high level to build credibility in my brand. These are a few extra steps I take to give me an edge while leading in a traditionally male-dominated role.

Karen Tokashiki

Director, Northrop Grumman Corporation

I think it is important for women to recognize that there are differences between men and women. These differences do not mean that you need to change to be more like a man; however, you do need to understand the differences and the language so that you can more effectively communicate and lead in a male-dominated workforce. Similarly to working in a foreign country, you should understand the different customs and respect the culture. Sometimes, women communicate in ways that come across as disrespectful to men, undermining their credibility or ability to influence without even realizing it. It is important for women to obtain a clear understanding of how they are being perceived by getting regular feedback from both men and women in the workplace. I've found that treating everyone with professional courtesy and building teams based on sound respect have been effective ways to influence and obtain support. Treating everyone with respect, and building and maintaining relationships are key to shaping your future. Being willing to take on new challenges, drive for execution, and display confidence are attributes important to your ability to lead and be perceived as a leader.

CHAPTER ~ 2 ~

TAKE
RISKS
AND
Learn
~ *from* ~
# MISTAKES

"I think I've learned much more about myself and how to be an effective leader when I've made mistakes or had a setback, than when everything has gone smoothly. **"**

Priya D. Bajoria

Group Manager (Client Services) & Associate Vice President, Infosys

---

In the words of Richard Branson, "If someone offers you an amazing opportunity and you're not sure you can do it, say yes – then learn how to do it later." Quite often, as women, we tend to be overly cautious, and will only raise our hand if we are 70 - 80% sure of having the right answer, or being the right candidate for a job, for example. We have to bridge that chasm and be willing to take more risks. Women also need to ask for a seat on the table more times than they usually do. However, we need to be prepared for what we can contribute if we do get offered that seat after all. In addition, in my experience, it is always essential to have a Plan B thought out, should you need to execute it at short notice.

Lisa Engel

Vice President New Product Development & Marketing, Emerson

During an interview, my prospective supervisor asked me, "Are you a five out of five, or a seven out of ten?" Luckily, this was during dinner, so I could chew my salad or sip my water to buy time. My mind raced. Engineers are expected to be right; why would he want to me to be right only 70% of the time? I would've been asked to leave the School of Engineering if that were the case, right? "Five out of five," I said confidently. He was looking for seven out of ten, and I knew it (I had just taken my first risk with him.) But I said it because, in the game of engineering, I love to win, and I hate to lose. I want to get every project right. I went on to explain the value of the seven out of ten philosophy. If we're not taking risks, albeit well thought-out risks, we're taking the safe road and not pushing the limits that drive creativity and innovation. Today, I actually appreciate evaluating failures. We spend an equal amount of time understanding failures as we do celebrating successes. Why? To learn, share and use the experience to make the next program even better.

Diane Foley

Sr. Director, Mission Assurance, Raytheon

There is one risk every woman should be willing to take – to stretch into their next role. Too often, women decide not to apply for a position, or self-select out of an exciting experiential opportunity because they haven't mastered 100% of the skills or knowledge necessary to be in that role. Yet, they'll scratch their heads when they see a man, not nearly as qualified, not only apply for that position, but actually get it. (There are actual gender differences behind this.) My advice is to take the chance. Sure, you may make a mistake or two, but chances are they will be relatively minor, and they will be the ones from which you learn the most. Stepping outside your comfort zone and challenging yourself is what makes you grow as a person and as a leader.

Rachel Heidenreich

VP of Quality & Continuous Improvement, Rockwell Automation

When I was about 10 years into my career, I had the opportunity
to take an assignment in Germany leading our European business
planning and marketing activities. This role was a risk: I had never
worked outside of engineering previously, let alone outside the US! In
addition, my husband necessarily had to leave his job, making me the
sole income earner for our family. With a husband and four daughters
onboard, we relocated to Duesseldorf, Germany. From a career
standpoint, it was extremely challenging: I was the only woman on
the leadership team, while being the least senior of the group. I found,
over time, that my inputs were not always heard, and that my role
was viewed more as a facilitator than a leader. Although thoroughly
enjoying the personal aspects of living in Europe, I definitely
thought I had made a misstep in my career, based on the struggles I
experienced in the office. In the end, after returning to the US three
years later, I found that, in the roles I held, I had learned a great deal
about business and global cultures supporting future success.

Andrea Karalus

Mechanical Design Discipline Chief, Pratt & Whitney

Every job transfer to a new position can be considered a risk. While working in my first engineering position, I realized I had different strengths relative to my peers. Although I was interested in the work, my instincts told me that in the long-term, this was not the best position for me. It took me six years to start looking at other job positions and to make an official request of my desires. Back then, there was not a well-defined job posting system. Because I spoke up, I was transferred to a totally new engineering discipline. I had stayed in my first engineering position for too long, and this taught me not to be afraid to act on my instincts. After that first transfer, my next targeted job transfer occurred in three years, incorporating what I had learned. That next position taught me vital skills that I needed, and set the stage for my career path. Realizing your natural strengths and setting a strategy for the skills you want to strengthen are the best things you can do when making career decisions.

Mariana Karam

Business Manager-Front End Equipment, Global Crop Harvesting Platform, Deere & Company

Do the Difficult. Great advice, but it means taking risks. After many highly successful engineering and leadership roles, I accepted an opportunity to work in Brazil. In 2001, it was still unusual for a woman in our company to be assigned a leadership role in emerging markets like South America. I was full of confidence and a sense of adventure. But, I quickly realized the challenge the assignment would represent. An organization with limited gender diversity, a completely different culture, and an urgent requirement to learn a new language all presented stress – even obstacles – to success. But in my eagerness to prove myself, I didn't seek the advice and help that would have made such a difference to the experience. Two years later, I left that assignment feeling like I had failed to make the impact I had hoped to achieve. But through coaching and reflection, I soon realized I had learned a very important lesson: Never be afraid to ask for help. Seek advice. Put aside pride, and have the confidence to admit "I don't know" – then find someone who does! I feel so lucky to have learned this lesson early in my career.

Ellen Kerr

Vice President, Operations Engineering Manager, FM Global

Be tenacious; often the difference between success and failure is tenacity. One of my favorite quotes is from Michael Jordan: "I've failed over and over and over again in my life, and that is why I succeed." As an example, I have been given opportunities to interview for roles where I wasn't considered the leading candidate. I never turned these chances down, regardless of the odds. One of the main reasons was that I always learned something, be it about myself, the role, the interviewer, etc. It also helped me prepare for the next time, which increased my odds at each successive attempt. Didn't get a job on the first try? Don't stress over it, learn from it. Reach out to the interviewer and get feedback on your performance. Many people don't take this step, and it is a critical part of the equation. We can't improve without understanding what needs to be modified and improved. Success doesn't come to those who wait for it, but to those who go after it.

Nan Mattai

Senior Vice President, Engineering & Technology, Rockwell Collins

---

Stretch beyond your comfort zone, and learn from your mistakes. We all have a so-called "comfort zone," that mental space where we live based on the boundaries we've set for ourselves. It's a place where we feel a sense of emotional security. When I look back, the younger me just wanted to do the best job I could, to be a good engineer. I was fortunate, though, that others recognized my potential and encouraged me to consider stepping outside my comfort zone and pursuing other roles. At first, I resisted because of the natural fear of the unknown. But eventually, I realized that these opportunities provided the means to grow and learn even more, to have a broader impact, and to gain a deeper understanding of the business and the company. It's a matter of balancing the excitement that the unknown can bring, along with the frustration and hardships we experience along the way. But the knowledge and experience we gain from the mistakes we make are what help us grow and improve by stretching our capabilities. We must always continue to challenge ourselves and those around us to be better tomorrow than we are today.

Maryann McNally

Vice President Innovation, ITW

A number of years ago, after being in the position for only a few months, I became responsible for several large projects. One of those projects, for a major customer, was seriously understaffed and in danger of not meeting a key customer deliverable. At the same time, our company had acquired some talent, and I was asked to meet with them to determine whether these employees should continue their employment. I met with the team and really liked their energy, enthusiasm, and teamwork. On a call with my manager, I indicated that I wanted to place the responsibility for my understaffed project in the hands of this new team. My gut told me this was going to work. My manager disagreed and indicated that he would not support this decision. But I persevered and essentially put my career on the line for that decision. This team knocked it out of the park, and we never looked back. And I learned to trust my instincts and not be dissuaded from making that risky decision.

Judy Moses

General Manager Asset Development,
MidContinent Business Unit, Chevron

People have often asked me if I have regrets, or if there are mistakes that I've made in my career. And the answer is "Of course!" I think I've learned much more about myself and how to be an effective leader when I've made mistakes or had a setback, than when everything has gone smoothly. A good example is my involvement in an acquisition a number of years ago. I came into the project as the project manager after the acquisition was complete. I essentially made the mistake of overly trusting all the work that had been done before and just executing the plan. Even though a few others warned that the assets couldn't deliver what we had planned, I didn't listen enough to those people and continued executing with predictably poor results. Through that experience, I learned a lot about what did and didn't work in my leadership style, and made a number of adjustments. I know I've been a much more effective leader in recent years as I've continued to be focused on execution, but also learned to listen to a wider range of viewpoints, and to both trust and verify the work products that employees bring forward.

Marla Peterson

Director, Engineering Operational Excellence, Honeywell Aerospace

---

I took on the deployment of a new software tool that would provide storage for all engineering data, analytical as well as computer aided design data. I worked and worked, but leadership decided to split the deployment into two parts. I felt that I had failed. But in reality, it sped up the deployment. I learned that, when you are too passionate about things, you can become a control freak. Leaders cannot afford to be control freaks. Delegation, developing, challenging workers, and ultimately giving and gaining their respect is being a leader. I realized early on that I was apologizing for everything! I said "Sorry" for everything. Even today, I have to consciously remember to not say "Sorry" unless I trip someone. I see other women say "Sorry" all the time, even if it's not because they ran into me. We need to not do that. We should not have to apologize for being present. I was told very early on that this is a sign of weakness. We need to own who we are, what we do, and we deserve to be engineers, managers, and leaders.

Emily Plunkett

Sr. Structural Engineer 3A, L-3 Communications

As a nervous college senior at a career fair, I accidentally made eye contact with a recruiter from a company I had not researched. He noticed my nametag with my major and engaged me in conversation. He read my resume and told me about the company. A few months later, I was invited to a site visit and interview in Texas. I knew that I could never live in Texas, but I thought it would be good to do a practice interview before the "real" interviews, so I accepted. During the visit, I found that the company was interesting and the atmosphere was exactly what I was looking for. The following week, they offered me a job as a Structural Engineer. I knew I could never settle in Texas, but I thought it would be a good idea to get some experience for my résumé, so I accepted. I figured that I would put in two years and then move on. That was over nine years ago. Since then, I have worked on a dozen interesting programs. I have been given opportunities to challenge myself both analytically and as a leader. What started as a "practice interview" has turned into a fulfilling career choice.

Margaret Simone

Senior Project Manager, Turner Construction Company

Early on, I was naive and thought that simply working hard and doing a good job were enough to reward me with success. I did not realize until much later that taking risks was required for success. Women like me falter because we are unclear which risks can make us the successful leaders we want to be. We lack role models in male-dominated fields, and the male approach to leadership and continued success doesn't always work for us. We tend to be more focused on the group at large and how we are perceived by or fit in that group than the success of us as individuals. We often don't want to appear unrealistic, and question our ability and worthiness, but we need to set the bar high in establishing our individual goals. However, developing relationships within our group by cultivating advocates, people whom you trust and who in turn promote you, is a key component in navigating the corporate ladder. Working to have these champions can feel risky at times, but they will help you continually reassess your circumstances and abilities. Success is about hard work, but establishing a strategy for achieving that is personal.

Patricia Solliday

Senior R&D Engineer, Boston Scientific

Being willing to take the not so glamorous assignments has proven to be an opportunity that propelled my career forward. Three years ago, I was asked to lead a stagnant project that lacked clear direction and had minimal management support. I had to overcome some opposition. There was quite a bit of change in the organization at the time, so the landscape was continually changing around me. However, with determination and consistent communication with management, the project was launched and successfully completed. This one project allowed an opportunity for my leadership competency to be put on display, despite multiple obstacles. Although it was not a large dollar project, the visibility to senior management created more project opportunities and recognition. These opportunities created networking connections that have proven valuable in the growth of my career.

Lauren Streb

Tech Transfer Lead, Genentech

Get to know the voices in your head. Yes, we all have them. Some of those voices sound like people from your childhood or mentors from your career. Others come from deep inside you. Understanding the voices – and when to listen to them – serves as an important compass when you evaluate taking risks. Which voices presented effective coping strategies for you in the past, but don't serve you now? Which voices are needlessly self-critical and should be ignored completely? I often struggle to review my personal history of successes and mistakes with objectivity. The paralyzing voice of my inner critic says not to expose myself to even the possibility of failure. When I find I am in that headspace, two strategies work well: 1) I imagine giving advice to someone else in my position, or 2) I remind myself of specific accomplishments and joys in my life that were only made possible by taking risks. After calming all that mental noise, I can evaluate the specific risk in front of me and make a choice, knowing that if I make a mistake this time, it will improve my decision-making down the road.

Melissa Tata

Director Engineering Program Management, Dell Inc.

I wanted to move into management quickly; however, I lacked experience, so I took an operations manager role, which was more typical for someone with several less years' experience than I had. Just six weeks later, there was a senior engineering manager opening, so I interviewed and was the third most promising candidate. I was asked to backfill the engineering manager role of the person who actually took the senior engineering manager role. Overall, I took a temporary step backward and attained a significant step forward in just six weeks by demonstrating how passionate I was about management, and by taking a risk to interview for a senior role for which I didn't have ample experience.

CHAPTER
~ 3 ~

EARN
what you DESERVE
AND
Enjoy
YOUR LIFE

" Your career is not a race to the finish line. It is a slow, steady climb integrated with your family and personal values. Your career should not define who you are. **"**

Decie Autin

Project Executive, ExxonMobil

Finding the right work life balance for me has been an evolution over my career, as I like to work hard and to play hard! Early in my career, I felt that I needed to downplay my need to leave the office to attend a child's school event or take them to the doctor. I was uncomfortable letting even my supervisor know I was out of the office on anything other than a work-related activity, so I would leave the light on and my briefcase in plain sight. Later on, I realized that I was doing a disservice to those coming behind me, and not being open about my ability to do my job AND take time to support my family. The company I work for developed a workplace flexibility program that encourages employees to take the time they need to support their children, their parents, and themselves, while keeping up with the demands of the business. Now, I am very visible about leaving the office to attend personal functions, and I encourage my staff to do the same. I hold myself accountable for getting my work done on time and for being where I need to be to support my family. It takes time and effort to plan, but it is worth it. I really enjoy my work, my family, and my vacations without the guilt I felt earlier in my career.

Priya D. Bajoria

Group Manager (Client Services) & Associate Vice President, Infosys

---

It is very important to make time for interests outside of work and family commitments. Whether it is traveling for pleasure, catching up with an old friend, discovering a new book or a restaurant that hasn't been written about yet, all of these help me feel refreshed and generate much-needed positive energy. As a leader, I have to stay motivated for my team to feel good. Having a happy mix of life within and outside work helps me build that strength inside me.

Lisa Engel

Vice President New Product Development & Marketing, Emerson

For many engineers and other STEM professionals, our college tenure combined with our careers will span a half-century. So it is very important to find a natural work/life balance designed specifically for you. Throughout my career, I've continued to solve this equation, and have been lucky enough to receive help from my family, friends, and neighbors. Yet, it hasn't been without a few mistakes along the way: a few missed school performances, early school drop-offs, and late pickups. And sometimes, it takes a gentle reminder to help me get back on track. A few years ago, my seven-year-old son was with me in my office after an early release school day. I gave him the usual doodle tools: highlighters, Post-it notes, and paperclips. You know the drill. He did a great job staying busy while I wrapped up and then shut down my computer. In my haste, I didn't notice the blue Post-it note he pasted on my door near my nametag. He signed the note, and I discovered it the following morning. It read, "My name is Lisa Engel and I work too much." Out of the mouths of babes. His note still hangs on my bulletin board.

Elizabeth Fuhrman

Associate Manager, Advanced Quality, Stryker

I prefer the concept of work/life integration. Working is a part of life; it is a portion of the 24 hours a day we have to live. To start, I ask myself, "What is my ideal work/life integration? What level of integration is needed for my enjoyment of life?" Everyone has a different need since we are motivated by different things. Some of us have kids and a husband; some of us have none. We have different aspirations for our careers or where we want to climb. What do you want? Decide on your goal, so you know where to head. Secondly, women need to understand the expectations of your organization. Is 8 to 5 a reality, or is there an unwritten expectation to stay till 6? Extreme research could leave you in the prospective company's parking lot at 5 to see how or when the parking lot empties. Lastly, I encourage women to communicate more effectively about what they complete and how it adds value vs. communication of a task list. The stereotype that men toot their own horn is sometimes true. Simply put, they are communicating their work, and we can mimic this while maintaining an effective to-do list.

Rachel Heidenreich

VP of Quality & Continuous Improvement, Rockwell Automation

I am an advocate for time management. That does not mean I am great at it, but I am always pursuing improvement, so that I can better achieve my priorities in life. Early in my career, I would at times feel like a victim with more work than I could accomplish during office hours. However, I would see colleagues be very successful, while working fewer hours than I was. I began to see that being successful was more about working on the critical items as well as effectively communicating results. I struggled with this, as I thought my hard work would be recognized without my pointing it out. Over time, I realized that I had to speak up in the appropriate settings. As a woman, I feel other women may also struggle with communicating their accomplishments. I learned with experience that communication is necessary to assure equity. For example, twice in my career I respectfully asked about my compensation and whether it was fair compared to my results and my peers. Both times, I was rewarded with substantive increases. These situations caused me to realize I had waited too long to speak up.

Andrea Karalus

Mechanical Design Discipline Chief, Pratt & Whitney

I think that engineers are generally programmed to define their goals over a certain timeframe, plan the strategy needed to accomplish those goals, and then execute them to meet the defined timeline. One could get so focused on this that she forgets to enjoy the ride getting there. In addition, one should always be mindful of the situation and recognize what one can change and what one cannot change. It is extremely important to be comfortable with your environment and, ultimately, with yourself. I have always focused on the career position and made sure that I was content and challenged by work assignments and goals. If I was not, then I learned to start searching for new job opportunities that fit into making me engaged and content. With that in mind, I have been extremely satisfied with what I have accomplished and the career path my life has taken. I always tell other young engineers that they really have to love their career and the people that they work with, and then the rewards and advancement will automatically come. I truly believe that.

Mariana Karam,

Business Manager-Front End Equipment, Global Crop Harvesting Platform, Deere & Company

---

"Work/life balance" has become such an important topic for both women and men in the workplace these past years. But I find myself using a different term to describe this aspiration: Harmony. I wasn't always sure of my credibility on this subject because I don't have children as part of the equation. However, two aspects of my life give me a story to tell. First, I have a husband who also works for John Deere, and who has an exceptional career of his own. Harmony can only be realized when there is mutual respect, support, and sometimes even sacrifice to ensure our life partners find joy and fulfillment. Second, I faced a health crisis several years ago that forced me to rethink my priorities and decide what really brought me happiness. That experience demonstrated that true harmony can only come from physical, mental, emotional, and spiritual balance. So, whether I'm making a decision about my work, family, health, or friends, I know all these elements must be aligned. When we navigate work and life decisions with a realistic understanding of both the rewards and tradeoffs, we find that making choices without regret is what brings the harmony we seek.

Susan Lewis

Vice President, Dow AgroSciences Operations,
The Dow Chemical Company

Work/life integration is a bit of a misnomer. Life is the whole of you.
It includes work, home, community, etc. As women, we sometimes
feel we have to be all, for all areas, all the time. That may be possible,
but not likely. Determine your focus for the situation, and make it your
best. For a period in your career, you may decide to work part-time
so you can spend more time with children, parents, or community,
etc. Other times, you may need or want to spend more time focused
on a specific project or position. It may be stressful to determine what
to do when faced with both. I found it very helpful to consult with my
husband, father, or other mentors. For a period in my career, after our
third child was born, I worked less than full-time. It was an opportunity
that worked well for us. You can look for examples where others faced
similar decisions with different paths. In the end, you will need to reflect
and make the best decision you can. Be the example for others, and
forge a new road if the option you want doesn't exist. Don't give up,
and be creative in ways you can make work for you.

Maryann McNally

Vice President Innovation, ITW

In today's global, fast moving environment, it is very hard to find work/
life balance. My daughters learned early on that to get Mommy's
attention, they literally had to take my face in their hands and make sure
we made eye contact so they knew they had my attention. Otherwise,
I was buried in emails, documents, and code. I answered emails in the
middle of the night. I would take a conference call whenever needed.
I would set aside and block out time slots in my calendar – time for
working out, or time for reflection – only to allow that dedicated
time to fill up with general meetings. So, I have always struggled to
disconnect from work. It is only late in my career that I have realized
that dedicating my life to work makes me less of the person I want
to be. So, after 30 plus years, I now hold fast to unplugging for one
whole day over the weekend. My work phone no longer sits on my
nightstand. And I take vacations seriously. I unplug and recharge. It is
up to you – you have to make the decision.

Marla Peterson

Director, Engineering Operational Excellence, Honeywell Aerospace

---

Establish a support structure at work and at home! At home, divide and conquer. We split everything: food preparation, groceries, laundry, caring for the boys, etc. If I need to stay late, my husband takes care of my part at home, and vice versa. We are a team. Find your teammates, and make a team. That includes work. Make sure your work team knows about you, and that they understand that family is important to you! In 1997, the University of Arizona (my alma mater) was playing Kentucky for the NCAA Basketball championship. A major meeting was called late in the afternoon of the day of the game. This meeting had our upper leadership reviewing our project. It started late, but since everyone knew that basketball was on my mind, I got to go first. The VP at the time even suggested that if anyone wanted to watch the game, they had better go. It helped that people know my passion at work and at home.

Sharon Rozzi

Senior Director Operations, Medtronic

As a wife and mother, my quest for work/life integration has been an adaptive process. I have not been afraid to break the status quo. Just prior to my first child, I was leading the number one project in my business, and my VP said, "Don't let the project slow down because of your leave." So I had team meetings at my home! I spent half the meeting time rocking or feeding the baby, but I had an agenda, the team brought results, and we moved the project forward. When I returned to work, I told my manager that I was going to take my lunch hour in two halves to nurse the baby who was at a nearby by child center. Her response was, "Do whatever you need to do." You can imagine my loyalty to her after that! My suggestions for young women engineers to achieve work/life integration is to insist on it. Don't be afraid to be a trailblazer. It only takes one person to tip the boat and establish new working norms. Also, be cautious of working for management that gauges your work by hours in the office, and not by whether objectives are met.

Jennifer Rumsey

Vice President of Engineering, Engine Business, Cummins

Unfortunately today, there are still places in our industry where men and women are not treated equally. Not only in terms of dollars, but also respect and value. If you feel you are in that situation, you have to be bold enough to have the conversation with your manager and own the responsibility of being treated fairly. Work/life integration is different for every person, so it's important to understand what is right for you. The first step is to determine goals for both your personal time and your professional time. If you only set professional goals, you'll only achieve professional goals. For me, balance means some level of sacrifice for both. Family is a big priority for me, and sometimes I miss a work function because of an important family commitment. At the same time, I sometimes miss things with my family because of work travel or other commitments. At the end of the day, you have to match the professional expectations of your career to the personal goals for your work/life integration. If you don't work for a company that allows you to find balance, then you are not going to be happy. Just don't be afraid to ask!

Vicky Saye

Vice President, Core Technology & Cost Optimization,
Kellogg Company

Whether we choose to admit it or not, committing to engineering as a career was destined to bring with it a certain level of intensity. It's how we choose to handle the intensity that makes all the difference. My philosophy is that work is a subset of my life. At times, it is certainly a bigger piece of the pie than it probably should be, but I have tried to manage that by focusing on the "big rocks." I've learned to compartmentalize when needed. If it's an important presentation or key point in a project, I'm at work to do my part. If it's an important game or recital, I'm there to cheer on my son or daughter. I have learned a valuable lesson – if the stars align such that there is something critical at home and something critical at work at the same time, home wins. There are people to back me up at work, but I am one of a kind in my family!

Margaret Simone

Senior Project Manager, Turner Construction Company

A career in construction is demanding and can require long hours. Initially, I found that I would leave my more tedious work to the end of the day when the phones were quieter and most people had left. But once I had kids, I wanted to be home, so I knew that work had to be done in the course of the workday. I felt it important to train myself to make the most of my time and be as efficient as possible. Focusing on my individual time management allowed me to do other things that were important to my professional life as well as my personal life. Having children is life changing for both men and women, but how to incorporate that event into a career seems daunting for a lot of women. I find that women worry about how that is going to happen well before the situation arises, but believing that it doesn't have to be career changing is an important part of a facilitating a more equal workplace with equal opportunities. If we prioritize what is important to us at a particular time, developing our own personal sense of normalcy keeps us balanced over time.

Patricia Solliday

Senior R&D Engineer, Boston Scientific

I think all of us women and men are trying to find a healthy work/life integration. What I have observed is that many of my male colleges do not internalize their work. While women seem to talk about the stresses at work and appear frustrated, the men seem to hit the gym and work out, or play ball at lunchtime or after work to deal with it. I believe the stresses are similar, but how we deal with them is different due to stereotypes and demographics. It is important to have a healthy balance. Corporations are now spending millions of dollars trying to help employees find a healthy work/life integration so their performance is enhanced. My advice is to enjoy all of the perks the company offers. There are times of high stress and long hours, but that should be equally balanced with enjoying the journey. Your career is not a race to the finish line. It is a slow, steady climb integrated with your family and personal values. Your career should not define who you are.

Karen Tokashiki

Director, Northrop Grumman Corporation

It is important to recognize that work/life "balance" is what works for you, AND is your choice. I made choices that allowed me to have the work/life balance that was right for me. When my children were young, my husband and I moved to a location close to work. This meant a smaller, older home; however, that allowed me to spend the time I needed at work as well as at home. I also chose career opportunities that did not require travel. It is important for you to ensure that your management has a clear understanding of your goals, capabilities, and successes, so that you are considered for new opportunities when they arise. It is also important to have a good support structure, both at home and work. When my children were young, I met regularly with a group of other young women engineers in a similar work/life situation, to discuss both personal and work issues. This support structure was key to providing balance in my life, and I can't say enough about the importance of women supporting other women. I also had a very supportive management structure that provided new opportunities. Through the years, as both my personal and professional life have changed, I have been able to make different choices that meet my definition of work/life balance. Now, I'm able to focus on supporting younger women through mentoring and providing opportunities for them.

CHAPTER
~ 4 ~

BE
CREATIVE
TO
create
CHANGE

"Learn to have the difficult conversation. Too often people don't want to confront known issues; they just learn to live with it. Good leaders understand it isn't easy, but is critical to constructive change and success.**"**

Decie Autin

Project Executive, ExxonMobil

I believe we need to treat each other as engineers, and not as female engineers or male engineers. Trying to change the status quo just for women can make men feel threatened and resentful. When I build a team, I look for engineers that have the right skillsets for the work, regardless of whether they are male or female. By building a team with members who have the right skills and the right personalities to allow them to work together effectively, I have been successful in working overseas in cultures where women are much more disadvantaged than they are in the USA. Those team members can come from multiple countries and different genders. The key to success is the synergies that are created when the right team comes together!

Lisa Engel

Vice President New Product Development & Marketing, Emerson

Change can be frightening, but it needn't be. Change can be a new hairstyle, a new home address, an evolving culture, a new job, or a promotion you're not quite ready for. Personal change is the most daunting of all. You may need to reeducate yourself for a career change, or transition into managing and motivating others, or maybe you have to become more corporate/politically savvy than ever before. Change will always come with uncertainty, but it doesn't have to come with fear. I redefine "change" to take the fear out of it. Change is challenge. Change is growth. Change is career-stretching. Yet, the most rewarding change in my life has been the privilege of helping others change. Whether it was volunteering with the Students in Engineering, Junior Achievement, or the Boys and Girls Club, I've always left with more in my personal toolkit than when I arrived. I would be remiss to not remind you to give back, as well. You see, I think John Ruskin was right when he said, "The highest reward for a person's toil is not what they get for it, but what they become by it." And isn't that the ultimate change?

Gayle Gibson

Director of Engineering, DuPont

I have seen women engineers excel when they place themselves in the customer's shoes to enable their teams to define and solve a problem. These individuals convey customer insight that serves as a "north star" to motivate work teams to take their internal "blinders" off, challenge the way things have always been done, and come together to deliver solutions that work for everyone involved. Engineers at DuPont are tackling challenges such as providing enough food for a growing population, building a secure energy future, and protecting both people and the environment. The magnitude of these challenges requires not only world-class technical skills and the ability to work with many internal and external partners, but a deep understanding of what our customers need and value. I encourage other women engineers to focus on gaining the trust of your colleagues and your customers by demonstrating empathy and championing the voice of the customer. Trust built on empathy is the connective tissue that allows a team to offer diversity of thought and ultimately deliver solutions that meet the customers' needs in a way no one single contributor can imagine.

Afsaneh Sunnie House

Vice President, Southwest Coast Sub Region Manager,
URS Corporation

I would find a way to eliminate the inferiority complex that many women have in the workforce. If every woman could learn to lean in and sit at the table, as Sheryl Sandberg suggests in her book *Lean In*, then we would have accomplished so much. The persona you present is the basis for how people form their perception of you. If you walk with confidence, dress for success, act like you belong, and sit at the table, people will form a more favorable opinion of you and your capabilities. A place to learn that confidence is at a professional women's organization like SWE. I have been involved in such organizations for 25 years, and it has been the best mentoring ground – where I can see and emulate female leaders. When I attend the conferences and meetings of these organizations, I get energized, encouraged, and motivated to be the best leader I can be. Women need more female role models at senior and executive levels in their own organizations. While the short-term exposure to these leaders at a conference is motivating, having access to those women in their own organizations is much more effective in combating that inferiority complex.

Mariana Karam

Business Manager-Front End Equipment, Global Crop Harvesting
Platform, Deere & Company

As engineers, we are known to be problem solvers. When I joined
John Deere over 20 years ago, my one ambition was to be a
powerhouse design engineer known as a technical leader in the
company. What I learned later is that we women engineers often have
natural talent to be powerhouse people leaders. We need to find more
ways to do that! Many engineers come to work each day thinking
about the next technical or design problem to solve. What if we came
to work every morning asking, "What can I do for the customer today?
What can I do for my employees and my business?" When I moved
from product development into operations roles – leading both wage
and salaried teams – I saw the focus visibly change from product to
people: team building, employee engagement, quality culture, and
business results centered around the customer experience. It was
a rare opportunity to lead teams that could have an impact on our
processes, work environment, and business results. And only through
active networking with colleagues across multiple functions beyond
engineering could we realize those results.

Ellen Kerr

Vice President, Operations Engineering Manager, FM Global

Embrace change, and look for ways to leverage it. Always look for ways to continually improve. What worked yesterday may not make sense today. Always ask yourself, "Is this adding value? Does the activity help the organization reach its goals?" Leaders empower everyone in the room to make decisions. A favorite quote from Lily Tomlin: "I always wondered why somebody doesn't do something about that. Then I realized I was somebody." Don't complain; look for ways to solve the problem. It may take experimentation and lots of failures before seeing success, but don't let it stop you. Learn to have the difficult conversation. Too often people don't want to confront known issues; they just learn to live with it. Good leaders understand it isn't easy, but is critical to constructive change and success.

Susan Lewis

Vice President, Dow AgroSciences Operations,
The Dow Chemical Company

One of my favorite quotes regarding change is: "Be the change you want to see." Many women have gone before us creating the change they wanted to see. We need to continue to do the same. If you want a more inclusive environment, then be more inclusive. If you want to gain respect, respect others. Look creatively at ways to include, recognize, and appreciate others. Be confident in your abilities, and create a positive energy around you. Don't wait or look only to others for changing a work/life experience. You have the power to do this. Be the leader, even if you aren't the supervisor. Talk with others on your team about your ideas, and listen to theirs. Likely, the diversity of ideas will create the changes needed professionally and culturally.

Judy Moses

General Manager Asset Development,
MidContinent Business Unit, Chevron

When I think about creating change, I immediately think of Noel
Tichy's book, which encourages every leader to have a "teachable
point of view." What this means to me is that successful leaders have
a strong vision for the business and what it takes to be successful.
They are able to convey this over and over again in different ways
to a variety of levels in the organization, and this ability is especially
important to accomplish change. Every situation where one needs
to accomplish change is different, but the common themes are
that one first needs to fully understand the problem, then develop a
clear vision of the solution. To be most successful, engage as many
stakeholders as possible – especially people who think differently
or have different backgrounds – and develop a "point of view" after
taking all that information into account. This approach has worked well
for me, particularly when I knew I needed to reorganize a group to
accomplish a shift in strategy. My having a strong point of view about
the need to change strategy and how to accomplish it eventually paid
dividends as we moved through the reorganization.

Marla Peterson

Director, Engineering Operational Excellence, Honeywell Aerospace

---

As leaders in an organization, we need to find the best talent or skillset. Being the example by having your resources' backs is extremely powerful to the entire organization. People seek you out so that they can work for you. One thing that I would change is removing the fear or threat of losing your competitive edge, and remember that we are all here working together. You need to be the change agent that shows that women are essential in any engineering environment. One of the most important changes necessary for women engineers to remember is that it's hard enough for women to work in a male-dominated profession, but women don't always work well with women. We need to promote, help, mentor, coach, and sponsor each other.

Sharon Rozzi

Senior Director Operations, Medtronic

The first thing I would change about the experience of the women engineers is the situation where women are on the sidelines and not contributing as much as they could because they are choosing to hold back. In my opinion, the most important thing women engineers need to do to gain respect professionally and culturally is to be courageous. Be courageous in pursuing your ideas and trying new approaches. Be courageous in failure, learn from it, and grow more capable. When you are a minority as a female engineer in the room, being courageous can be scary because of the visibility you have as a minority. When I am in a meeting and I see women on the sidelines who I can tell have something to contribute, I reach out to bring them into the dialogue. Through my company's internal SWE network, and through women's peer mentoring circles, I have been able to foster environments where women can speak out and be courageous in sharing their ideas with other women as practice for being courageous in their day to day work environment.

Jennifer Rumsey

Vice President of Engineering, Engine Business, Cummins

The reality in our world is that cultural expectations of women are extremely challenging. Each woman needs to define the right path for her and not be afraid to challenge the cultural norms. In my family, my husband and I have swapped the traditional primary caregiver role, which is becoming more common, but still counter to what society expects. Often at speaking events, I will have younger women ask me what I do to be "less female" in the workplace. I point out NOTHING. I am true to myself, and that does not make me any less capable than my male counterparts. I don't feel compelled to wear a blue shirt and khaki pants to work, but dress in tasteful and stylish feminine clothes. I may show more care and compassion to my team than some of my male counterparts, but that is a part of who I am. Of course, you have to be professional in a corporate environment, but I think it's another example of the value that diversity brings to a team.

Margaret Simone

Senior Project Manager, Turner Construction Company

Young women engineers today talk to me about the struggles and challenges of their everyday work life. These discussions are rarely about the technical aspects of the work itself, and more often about personal interactions and relationships and how to manage those situations with authority. There are some in that group who find it hard to overcome situations they feel they never come across in their personal life in dealing with men. We need to trust our instincts when dealing with them. If something doesn't feel right, it probably isn't. If you don't like something that is said or done, you need to figure out your personal approach to address it. Be it personal or professional, handling these issues with poise allows you to focus on the work and not the differences in gender. Sitting at the table is a popular mantra these days. Don't be afraid or intimidated to take your seat.

Patricia Solliday

Senior R&D Engineer, Boston Scientific

Generally, across multiple corporations, my peers often discuss the gender specific salary gap. In my opinion, it often appears that women work harder to achieve the same or less recognition and salary of their male counterparts. If there were a transparent way to narrow the gap between the average salaries of male versus female equivalents, we would take a step in the right direction. Too many career minded women feel the pressure to outperform their male peers by working longer, harder, and taking extra projects, only to achieve slightly less reward. This creates an unfair expectation of new women entering into this type of environment. I would change this norm within the corporate environment, level the playing field, and be intentional about closing the gender specific salary gap.

Karen Tokashiki

Director, Northrop Grumman Corporation

One of the most exciting change opportunities I have had is developing and running a program to develop women in leadership. The objective of the program is to grow and connect a network of technical women across the organization, ready to take on larger leadership roles. The program consists of workshops, team projects, mentoring, and networking with executives. Workshops are focused on improving communication and presentation styles, negotiation, and business and politically savvy skills. The leadership components are focused on helping the women gain respect both professionally and culturally in a male-dominated workforce. Each session concludes with networking events, which provides the opportunity for the women to gain visibility with executive leadership. The women work together on projects, further building their relationships. And they present their projects to the Leadership team, using skills learned throughout the course. The program has continued to evolve and improve through feedback and support from the women graduates. The feedback has been extraordinary, and the most gratifying reward is watching as the women obtain and move into new opportunities of greater influence, and create a visible change in the workforce.

CHAPTER
~ 5 ~

ESTABLISH
and
EVOLVE
YOUR
brand

" As you gain knowledge throughout your career, you will
be perceived differently but the heart of who you are will
likely not change. Your intellect, values and ethics will guide
you in your brand development. **"**

Priya D. Bajoria

Group Manager (Client Services) & Associate Vice President, Infosys

---

Inside the workplace, I am known for my deep domain experience in financial services and my ability to leverage that to design and implement innovative solutions for clients. I am also recognized for a strong work ethic, and a willingness to take on new challenges and the hard work that goes behind making those initiatives a success. I am known as a diversity champion, and I am actively involved in initiatives that involve giving back to the communities we operate in. Outside of work, my friends know me as someone who has varied interests and lives life to the fullest. This personal brand has held me in good stead, and also guides me when I need reaffirmation of my own value proposition. It requires consistent effort to establish and maintain one's personal brand, and social media can be effectively leveraged toward this objective.

Lisa Engel

Vice President New Product Development & Marketing, Emerson

We all have one: a friend or family member who is the iconic "glass half empty" type. I avoid them. I'm sure they never planned to be a "pill" that could only be tolerated in small doses. Yet, you are responsible for "this brand called YOU." So, what are your brand attributes? How do your colleagues describe you? While uncomfortable, I encourage you to seek input from your peers and coworkers. I participated in a 360-degree performance review assessment once, and the results sent me on a mission. The results indicated that I wasn't a good listener. Who are these people? I'm a great listener. When I peeled back the onion, layer by layer, I discovered my tendency to finish people's sentences. That means I started talking (and solving the problem) before the speaker finished speaking. Guilty as charged. So now, I'm cognizant of this tendency, and make a concerted effort to sit still, take notes, and just listen. You see, my personal brand is still evolving. And it was a great day for me when I realized that it was more satisfying when the solution did not come out of my mouth — but rather from someone I was patient enough to listen to.

Diane Foley

Sr. Director, Mission Assurance, Raytheon

"I work harder than anyone else on my team. I am one of the top performers, and whenever there's a really tough problem, people come to me to solve it. My boss will notice, and eventually I'll get the promotion I deserve. Right?" Not necessarily. In a perfect world, those who performed the best would receive the most recognition. They would move up the ladder faster than their peers and get the biggest raises. But life is far more complicated. To move ahead, people need to be able to see you in your next role. If you are perceived as a "reliable, detail-oriented, hard worker," people may not see you as the "strategic, creative, thought leader" for whom they are looking. That's the importance of your brand. Consider the next step you'd like to take in your career. Think of the three adjectives you'd like used to describe you in that position. Now work on making the perception of you match the reality. Help others to see you were thinking ahead five years as you developed your solution set. Highlight the creative way you overcame the huge obstacles you and the team faced. Use your "brand" to make things happen for you.

Lynda Grindstaff

Director of Innovation Solutions - Intel Security Group,
Intel Corporation

My reputation and work ethics have created my personal brand.
Very early in my career, one of my mentors told me that I didn't have
a brand and needed to establish one. He said that I would go far
if everything I touched turned to gold. I have tried to live by that as
much as possible by doing every job with high quality and leaving
people with a good impression of me. If you are just establishing your
brand, or are not sure what your brand is, I recommend thinking about
how you want others to perceive you, and then live that way. Also,
have people you trust start to speak about you in a positive light to
create a positive reputation. What do you think your personal word
cloud would say if you asked all your friends and colleagues for three
adjectives that best described you? If the words that showed up aren't
what you would like to see, then it's time to change your brand.

Rachel Heidenreich

VP of Quality & Continuous Improvement, Rockwell Automation

Early in my career, I felt like my personal brand was "the girl in the meeting," as I spent much of my working life being the only female in virtually every professional setting. I spent a lot of time trying to avoid typical female attributes: I would not wear pink to work, paint my nails, or talk about shopping or doing crafts. Over time, I found that there can be an advantage to being different; it seemed that others might listen more closely to my statements, and most people knew who I was. Thankfully, the workplace has improved in its tolerance to differences and even, at my current employer, celebrate the differences and the value they bring. So at this point, my style has evolved to being much more myself in my work interactions. I even admit I love to shop and cross-stitch. I also share my experiences with younger women in the workplace in the hopes that they do not need to go through this process of hiding their personality in the workplace. I find that being more open about myself helps my confidence, and I enjoy work the work I do much more.

Andrea Karalus

Mechanical Design Discipline Chief, Pratt & Whitney

I do not particularly perform specific actions or say specific statements to differentiate myself from the crowd. I feel that the role of today's engineer has changed. The world needs engineers who can function as problem solvers and who have the insight to act on setting procedures for problem avoidance. Today's generation needs to develop more collaborative skills, and they need to be good communicators. The best way for an engineer to succeed is to develop skills that will help her manage for the long term. Once you have a known track record as a collaborative leader, and you have successfully shown that you know how to work with others to solve or avert issues that are important to your particular business, then you have established your brand.

Ellen Kerr

Vice President, Operations Engineering Manager, FM Global

Be true to yourself. You will grow and evolve with each step in your career. Remember along the way what gives you joy and brings fulfillment. When you stay the course and be true to your ideals, you will be passionate. This passion is what makes a difference and will resonate with others. The ideals and passion become part of your brand. For me, regardless of my role, I find joy in seeing people reach their maximum potential. I have tried to find opportunities to help do this regardless of my role. At the end of the day, this is what resonates for me and I what consider part of my brand.

Susan Lewis

Vice President, Dow AgroSciences Operations,
The Dow Chemical Company

It is important to think about what you represent and how you want to be perceived. This is part of personal branding. Over time, perception of women engineers has evolved and your brand will too. As you gain knowledge throughout your career, you will be perceived differently but the heart of who you are will likely not change. Your intellect, values and ethics will guide you in your brand development. As a young engineer, I noticed that women dressed or tried to act more like men and didn't differentiate themselves or stay true to what they believed. In the past few decades though, we have seen progress. Women have achieved great results and high positions with an overarching brand of professionalism without being afraid to be themselves.   In the end, that is the easiest and best part of what we all can bring to the table. When we are comfortable with ourselves, we are free to contribute at the highest levels and lead confidently.   Your personal brand will shine through.

Judy Moses

General Manager Asset Development,
MidContinent Business Unit, Chevron

For me, "brand" is synonymous with reputation. You build your reputation over your entire career. Many of the people you meet, either in your company or in your industry, will reappear again over the course of your career, so even small interactions can build or hurt your reputation. A critical success factor in building your brand is understanding what characteristics your company and industry most need, and developing your skills, competencies, and ultimately your reputation in that area. My experience in both my own career, and in observing many other technical careers in the oil and gas industry, is that being known early-career for work ethic, teamwork, and technical diligence, as well as the willingness to take on additional tasks, is critical to obtaining additional career opportunities. Whether you're interested in a technical career path or a leadership career path, you will later need to be known for willingness to mentor and lead others, and an ability to respond well to any challenge given to you. If you aspire to general manager and higher leadership positions, evolving your skillset and reputation to include an ability to manage people, manage a financial business, and clearly communicate with a variety of audiences is critical.

Sharon Rozzi

Senior Director Operations, Medtronic

My brand has been built from my work results and the behaviors people observe in me. My brand has been built by being self-aware of my strengths, and being deliberate about seeking roles that exploit and develop them. For example, one of my strengths is my analytical capability. I have sought roles where I can solve difficult problems through rigorous data analysis. Each time my colleagues see me do this, it builds equity in my brand. With online strength assessment tools, I am seeing more women be self-aware of their strengths and able to articulate their value proposition. However, for the brand to resonate with colleagues, you have to fulfill the brand promise every day by demonstrating those strengths through observable behaviors. Women are frequently perceived as not being capable of leading in business critical situations because their brand is perceived as risk averse. Indeed, there is evidence that women are appropriately risk averse by preventing fires in the first place. My advice to women on breaking through this bias is to find ways to demonstrate leadership on progressively larger issues. Management must also be self-aware of biases they have on this topic and seek to overcome them.

Jennifer Rumsey

Vice President of Engineering, Engine Business, Cummins

Thinking about what you want your brand to be is important. What do you want to represent, and how will you exhibit this in the work you do? As an example, when I think about my own brand, I think about the following things I work to represent:

- **Strong promoter of diversity**

- **Caring leader who cares about people and people development**

- **Creates a trusting environment of open communication. Brings teams together, and ensures issues are raised and addressed effectively**

- **Sees and understands the big picture and how to make the business better**

The core challenge for women building their brands can be the cultural lens through which people view men and women. You have to be confident and stand behind what you believe. Too many women are encouraged to move away from technical leadership roles. You can't move into a peripheral role like program management or marketing if you want to grow inside a technical field. If you allow yourself to be pushed out of technical roles because you're perceived differently, then your opportunities for technical roles will shrink.

Margaret Simone

Senior Project Manager, Turner Construction Company

It is easy to understand that the technical aspects of the work are an important set of skills we need to advance, but learning how to be a leader is a skill that deserves our equal attention. We tend to think that will come to us with time, but the evolving process of determining the kind of leader you want to be starts on day one. It is obvious to us which bosses or persons of power we either do or do not want to emulate, and we should be editing those tactics and techniques into our practice. Visualizing ourselves in positions of power and how we want to behave when we get there is something very personal and so important. Whether it is the rigors of the workday, the lack of female leaders, or the perceived lack of opportunity, we tend to lose sight of the importance of developing our leadership role. There is an expectation that women engineers will not be future leaders, but rather, future mothers, so acting the part early on leaves our options open for whatever we decide.

Patricia Solliday

Senior R&D Engineer, Boston Scientific

I am continually working on my personal and professional brand. Diversity seems to be integrated in everything I do. There are many types of diversity that organizations can capitalize on. I have used myself as a strong diversity change agent in my organization to create opportunities for others while I am advancing my career. I am always networking to increase my circle of influence, so I can develop a critical mass and execute change quickly when necessary. I have learned that taking time to build authentic relationships will have a return on investment that is immeasurable. I believe my professional brand has given me an opportunity to sit at many tables to influence change.

Melissa Tata

Director Engineering Program Management, Dell Inc.

I have changed roles on average every 15 -18 months, and I never really had lengthy formal interviews, but rather relied on my reputation and recommendations from my coworkers and leadership. I demonstrated that I have strong learning agility, and can build a strong team to complement my skills. I have always dressed for the role I wanted next vs. business casual like many of my peers. I've found that assertiveness is better respected from men; however, the best women leaders have learned how to do this effectively.

Karen Tokashiki

Director, Northrop Grumman Corporation

The first step in establishing your brand is your performance, demonstrating that you are a high performing employee making valuable contributions toward the business objectives. However, I don't think women spend enough time thinking about what their brand truly is, or how they might influence how they are perceived through specific actions. Women may expect others to just see and recognize their capabilities vs. learning how to communicate effectively in order to obtain the roles and new opportunities they desire. I believe women are sometimes perceived as less technical, and may not be perceived as drivers of execution vs. their male counterparts. They may gravitate toward organizational, support roles vs. highly technical or program management roles. This may also be a result of supporting their work/life balance. However, in order for women to achieve the same leadership roles as their male counterparts, they must work to change these perceptions. Helping women to obtain visibility with male and female leaders who will consider them for greater leadership roles is important to influencing this change. And as more women achieve executive roles, these perceptions will start changing.

CHAPTER ~ 6 ~

ADVICE
to my
YOUNGER
☆ Self ☆

"Stop yourself from making assumptions about what someone else is thinking; often what we assume we hear is what we are telling ourselves.**"**

Decie Autin

Project Executive, ExxonMobil

My Dear Decie, You are in the middle of you career, and you have come so far! Your family is very proud of your accomplishments, and you should be, also. Seize the day and continue addressing challenges head-on as you work toward your goals. Your empathetic approach to understanding the issues and developing mitigations is effective. Remember that there is never a straight line to where you want to go, so keep your mind open to opportunities that you may have never anticipated – they may take you places you can't imagine now. Also, remember to always take time for your family and friends, for they have always supported you and have been key to who you are today. Avoid those that would minimize your accomplishments to make themselves feel better. Don't doubt yourself or your intuitions. You have a track record that proves you can do anything you put your mind to, so continue to capitalize on those strengths. As you enter the second half of your career, consider the legacy that you would like to leave both at work and beyond, and start planning. Your success will continue, and you can feel good about where you are going. Sincerely, Your Retired Self.

Priya D. Bajoria

Group Manager (Client Services) & Associate Vice President, Infosys

---

Find a mentor/champion in the workplace; they may not always come looking for you. Make sure you are contributing something to that relationship to make it worth their while to continue to invest and believe in you. Don't be afraid to take risks; you are going to do all right. Open your mind to new possibilities; the sooner you explore them the better. Take time to cherish yourself; when a woman becomes her own best friend, life becomes easier.

Liz Buzzard

R&D Scientist, The Clorox Company

One thing I wish I would have known when I first started working is the importance of feedback. In your job, you will be evaluated on your accomplishments and actions, not on your intentions. Having an open dialogue with your boss, project managers, and peers about things you are doing well and things you need to improve upon will allow you to correct mistakes quickly instead of repeating them. Ask your boss and others you work with for feedback regularly so they are comfortable giving it to you. Receiving negative feedback is tough. When you do receive negative feedback, try not to react defensively, and think of it as an exercise in identifying ways to be more successful at your job.

Marietta Cleveland

Quality Center Manager, Chrysler Group LLC

Don't be afraid to be who you truly are. Explore different opportunities early in your career so that you have a broader perspective of the things that are available to you. Find your voice and speak up. Don't take things personally, they'll only cause you to doubt yourself. Stay positive because life is a journey and should be enjoyed both at work and outside of work. Have people in your inner circle that are supportive and have a positive outlook on life. Always give back and help others. Share your failures and successes with others so that you can help them to learn from your experiences.

Diane Foley

Sr. Director, Mission Assurance, Raytheon

"They are lucky to have someone like you working for them." If I could go back in time, that's what I'd tell myself. So much of my career I have spent grateful to have a job – grateful to have been "chosen" and then tolerated despite my shortcomings. In my mind, all my imperfections were magnified. I really felt that, someday, someone would realize I really didn't have all the requisite qualifications for the job, and I'd be fired, or at least pushed aside. Imagine my surprise when I realized I wasn't the only one. That, in fact, there was a name for what I was feeling: the Imposter Syndrome. In some ways, it was a relief to know that. But intellectually knowing something doesn't necessarily change the way you feel every day. And while I could look back and wonder what opportunities I missed while I was afraid, I know that it was those feelings of inadequacy that drove me to be better, to learn more, and to strive for more than my colleagues. They drove me to a higher standard for myself and for others. They made me a better employee, a better teammate, and, ultimately, a better leader.

Lynda Grindstaff

Director of Innovation Solutions - Intel Security Group,
Intel Corporation

If I was to give advice to my younger self, I would tell myself to actually get several mentors and sponsors early in my career to help chart the course ahead. I always thought, "Someday I'll get a mentor or a sponsor..." but before I knew it, someday had come and gone and I was stalled in my career. Fortunately, the stall didn't last too long, as I did begin to utilize mentors and sponsors more. This paid off by them encouraging me to take risks and try things outside my comfort zone. My other bit of advice to my younger self is: "NO IMPOSTER SYNDROME!" (And yes, that is yelling.) I had the classic case of imposter syndrome, and as my husband can testify, it came out every year, especially around the annual performance review cycle. I would dread my reviews, and always felt I was never good enough. Fortunately, my reviews were always good, but it still wasn't enough to shake the imposter syndrome. I finally did shake it when I won a SWE Emerging Leader Award, and realized, "I do deserve to be here!"

Rachel Heidenreich

VP of Quality & Continuous Improvement, Rockwell Automation

As a mom of four daughters, I remember being stressed about balancing my work and personal life. At the time, I was in a role in Germany with a long commute, and what seemed to be unending responsibilities. While putting my seven-year-old to bed one evening, I was telling her how worried I was about all the work I had to do. She responded with, "Just figure out what's most important, Mom, and do that." If I could give advice to my younger self, it would be to take that advice early on in my career, rather than feeling the stress and worry of trying to accomplish everything. Although it is easier to say than do, a healthy balance between family, faith, and work helps keep it all in perspective.

Afsaneh Sunnie House

Vice President, Southwest Coast Sub Region Manager,
URS Corporation

I had wanted to be an engineer since the 7th grade. It was my father's
dream, and it became my dream. I am very happy with my career
choices, but I did not choose wisely at the start of my career. Although
the job market was very tough in the early 1980s because of the
recession, I passed on interviewing with California Department of
Transportation (Caltrans) before I graduated. I did not know much
about the transportation industry, and did not think it was for me. I
finally applied at Caltrans, and was hired after two years of looking
for work. I have been in this field now for 30 years. I would advise my
younger self to embrace the journey I was about to take, stay open to
the many opportunities that would come my way, and rest assured that
the instincts that have served me so well thus far in life would continue
to be a reliable foundation upon which I would build my career. I would
also advise myself to get a mentor from the engineering profession
while I was in college, so I could better understand the industry and
what it had to offer.

Stacy Johnson

Americas eMarketing Manager, Agilent Technologies

My first cooperative education assignment was at a startup company specializing in alternative fuels. My job responsibilities included making coffee, answering phones, transcribing an Italian engineer's thoughts from cassette tapes into softcopy, and I occasionally acted as a button-pusher for a tester. It was the longest summer of my life! I was so bored. Years later, I was working for a different startup company where I dealt with international people frequently over the phone. It was during a call with some Europeans that I realized that the transcription task for an Italian engineer with a heavy accent might have been the single-best learning experience of my younger life. I had learned how to listen! Every situation presents itself for a reason. If we take the time to look for the good in it and try to make the most out of it, the reason will show up.

Dr. Ruth Jones

Mishap Investigation Specialist, NASA Safety Center

I would advise every girl who wants to become an engineer to take all the math and sciences classes you can while in high school and do well in these classes. As you get into the upper level math and science classes, you will probably be the only girl in the class, but this is only preparing you for the male-dominated field you are about to enter as an engineer. I remember when I was in high school, I would compete with the guys in my class to get the highest grade, and my teacher would count my problem wrong if I left off the negative sign. He would always say, "That negative sign could've blown up the space shuttle." I thought, "I had the right answer, I just left off the negative sign," but my teacher was very adamant about that. That analogy stuck with me forever, and ironically I got a job with NASA. If girls take their math and science classes seriously while in high school, they will excel in college and in the workforce as female engineers.

Andrea Karalus

Mechanical Design Discipline Chief, Pratt & Whitney

Some advice I would give my younger self is to explore as many varied, available career opportunities as possible. This will broaden one's resume early in your career. This means potentially moving out of your comfort zone more often, which is much easier to do when one is young and has fewer responsibilities. As a young engineer out of school, you are not expected to know everything, and it is better to ask questions and interact with as many mentors as possible. Making these decisions early in your career builds your connections and is definitely what you need as you advance in your career.

Mariana Karam

Business Manager-Front End Equipment, Global Crop Harvesting Platform, Deere & Company

---

Imagine yourself watching your own funeral. What will people say about you? And what would you WANT them to say about you? Early in my career and life, I would have wanted to know that it will ultimately be about PEOPLE and relationships. No one will talk at my funeral about the patents I filed, deadlines I beat, or promotions I earned. They'll talk about how I made a difference to the people I knew or touched. I would want advice to BE CONFIDENT in my capabilities, my value, and my knowledge. But being confident doesn't mean we know everything. Never be afraid to ask for advice or help. And plan to BE GENEROUS in sharing experiences – both successes and failures – so others can learn and develop. This can be tough when you are ambitious and focused on defining and growing your own career. But the relationships you build through this goodwill will be based on a respect and trust that can be rare in our competitive, technically-focused industry. As long as I keep learning and living these lessons, I still feel like my younger self!

Ellen Kerr

Vice President, Operations Engineering Manager, FM Global

You would be amazed at what you are capable of doing! Listen to your gut; it won't steer you wrong even when everyone around you is telling you to do something different. Enjoy each step of the journey, knowing there will be both bad and good. Learn from the bad, and cherish the good!

Susan Lewis

Vice President, Dow AgroSciences Operations,
The Dow Chemical Company

The advice I would give my younger self is pretty simple and really common sense. As engineers and leaders, we continue to evolve and respond to different situations, teams, and people. Sometimes it can be tough and frustrating but these bullets tend to remind me to get back to the basics and focus on the simple answers.

- **Trust your intuition. It will almost always lead you down the right path. It may not be the easiest path or the one with instant results but in the end will likely be the right decision**

- **Don't worry about what others think. Be yourself - you don't need to be like the men and women before you.**

- **Focus on teamwork and collaboration to confidently deliver results while forging the path ahead**

Nan Mattai

Senior Vice President, Engineering & Technology, Rockwell Collins

---

Believe in yourself and your abilities. As a young woman, I was good at math and science, but never imagined becoming an engineer. There were no women engineer role models around me, so I pursued advanced degrees in physics to become a research scientist. But things didn't work out as planned. My first son came along, and I did not complete graduate studies. I was at a crossroads, trying to decide what to do next when two amazing people in my life provided me with the advice and support I needed. My mother, a woman without a college education, always encouraged me to dream big, work hard, and never accept that something can't be done. In that moment of uncertainty, her words reminded me that I couldn't give up – not then or ever. Then, my husband, Roy, who is also an engineer, encouraged me to consider engineering. He thought I'd be good at it, based on my education and problem solving skills. Looking back, he believed in my abilities more than I did at the time. So, recognize the skills that you have and the good things about yourself – there are many! You may not always see them, but they are there.

Maryann McNally

Vice President Innovation, ITW

Follow your passion, and don't let anyone talk you out of it. Try very hard to discover yourself – know what you are good at, know what you need to work on yourself, and be honest with your self-appraisal. Do not be afraid to speak your mind. Trust your instincts. With every opportunity, work hard and make sure it is a learning opportunity. Raise your hand when new opportunities present themselves – even if they are scary. They are usually the most valuable learning experiences in your career arc. Always, always have fun. Do not let work consume you. While your career is an important and vital part of your life, the most crucial thing to remember is that it is only a part of your life. Engage in your community, stay connected with friends, and maintain a healthy and vibrant network of colleagues.

Judy Moses

General Manager Asset Development,
MidContinent Business Unit, Chevron

I'd offer the following advice to my younger self: Push yourself to have the courage of your convictions, give voice to those convictions, and go outside your comfort zone with assignments and roles. I wouldn't be where I am today except for a colleague that I worked with early in my career. Her personality was different to mine, and she helped me realize that being more aggressive about speaking up and pushing for what I believe in and being willing to try all sorts of new things were critical to having an enjoyable and rewarding career. This comes up in many practical ways – I often think of this advice when I'm offered a new opportunity or assignment that I haven't imagined myself in before. For example, taking a lateral move to Indonesia and going well outside my comfort zone was one of the best things I've done for my career because it allowed me to demonstrate that I could be successful in a variety of roles and cultures. I've also found that, even though I'm essentially an introvert, I am ultimately happier at work when I know that I've spoken up on the issues that I feel strongly about and have made my thinking clear.

Marla Peterson

Director, Engineering Operational Excellence, Honeywell Aerospace

---

Absorb everything quickly. Take some risks. Learn everything about the company you work for. Volunteer – always be the first one through new training. Watch the battles you take on – make sure they count, and don't take on all the battles. Learn from your leaders: anticipate their actions and their questions. Take it all in and be you! And have fun!

Emily Plunkett

Sr. Structural Engineer 3A, L-3 Communications

If I could give advice to my younger self it would be to ask questions. When I started my job right out of college, I was shy and very intimidated by the engineers working around me. Another new college graduate – a male engineer - started the same day as me. He spent the first couple weeks asking his mentor questions and regularly getting coached on each assignment. I was so shy and quiet that I treated each assignment like a test, to be graded when I was finished. I feel that if I had asked more questions early on, I would have had a much better foundation and a much quicker transition into becoming a productive member of the engineering team.

Sharon Rozzi

Senior Director Operations, Medtronic

My advice to my younger self would be to be courageous in going after roles you want and seeking stretch opportunities. I would go back to age 17 at the time I was choosing a university. I was accepted to Cornell as freshmen, but somehow I talked myself into attending a less prestigious school because I didn't think I could handle Cornell. I went elsewhere and found myself bored. Realizing my mistake, I transferred to Cornell for my sophomore year. Yet, I made the error again my first year in graduate school at age 22. I wanted to pursue an area of graduate studies that was very intensive in mathematic modeling, but there were no women in the program. I allowed myself to be intimidated and choose a different research area. I paid the price with four years of research on a topic I was not passionate about. If I could go back in time and talk to my younger self, I would give her the pep talk I have given my own seventeen-year-old daughter on several occasions: to go after what you want and don't be afraid to test the limits of what you are capable of.

Jennifer Rumsey

Vice President of Engineering, Engine Business, Cummins

Today, my career perspective is similar to Cheryl Sandberg's quote that: "Careers are a jungle gym, not a ladder." There are many women I met studying engineering at Purdue or early in my career who have since left the technical field, especially when they started their families. In hindsight, I wish I'd done more to encourage them to stick to their careers and find ways to make it work. There are lots of options, including working part-time, hiring help, and more equally balancing work between partners. In reflecting on my own career decisions, there is little I would change. The decisions I made about moving between companies early in my career, and then to different roles within Cummins, have been the right ones for me. As a result, I have an exciting and rewarding role as one of the senior technical leaders at Cummins. I've learned along the way not to try to predefine a path or how you're going to make everything work in life, but to constantly learn, evaluate, and adjust what you're doing and the direction you are headed.

Vicky Saye

Vice President, Core Technology & Cost Optimization,
Kellogg Company

Simply put, be in the moment. We are all so busy that our lives flash before us in the form of an Outlook calendar. Take the time to listen to people, understand the impact of decisions, and do the right thing. Continue to build leadership and technical skills, and don't hesitate to step up. It's about the journey – the people, the experience, the decisions, the impact. Bottom line, if you're waiting to get to the destination to enjoy life, you might be surprised that it's not what you imagined it to be. The best part was the process of getting there!

Margaret Simone

Senior Project Manager, Turner Construction Company

I once had a teacher say, "Don't ever sell yourself short." She was older and quirky, so the words did not resonate with me until much later. Studying engineering and having no construction experience, I was cautious to not expose that, and in doing so I underestimated myself. I had to overcome that self-doubt. My motivation was building a successful project, and I am lucky that it is something that I love to do. But that in itself was enough to be recognized and succeed. Making your mark, making a difference, figuring out how you are going to make your impact, and the importance of it I learned very late. Don't be afraid to take what you are good at and what you love to do and develop that into who you want to become. Don't let the confines of the "job" limit your potential. Trust your instincts, and act on them. It doesn't always work, but when it does, the rewards are worthwhile.

Patricia Solliday

Senior R&D Engineer, Boston Scientific

If I could do it over again, I would start at my first job out of college. I would enjoy the journey of life, instead of pressing for the next promotion, realizing there are no shortcuts to a successful career. I would learn as much as I could in the place I was and try not to rush through to the next job. I would build and maintain professional relationships, and continually add people to the list weekly. I would take people management classes to understand how to leverage diverse talent of all kinds. I would host and attend more casual networking parties to understand what other people are doing in their life and not be so self-centered in my own career. I would have started the MBA program five years after working in industry, instead of 15, so I could leverage what I learned and maximize my career sooner. I would be intentional about living life to its fullest in every area: spirituality, family, children, travel, community, hobbies, and wellness. I think if someone would have tried to give me the advice I am trying to give my younger self today, I am not sure that I would have realized what a gift this advice is. Hindsight is always crystal clear. My final words are dig deep and try to understand "who you are" before throwing yourself into a career. Give yourself permission to change paths if needed. Life is a journey, not a race.

Jean Bennington Sweeney

Vice President Environment, Health, Safety and
Sustainability Operations, 3M

Looking back on my career, I realize that, in the first ten to fifteen
years, I took everything too seriously. I thought many of the things
I saw were a personal slight toward me or an act of disrespect.
Because I was so focused on being a successful woman in a male-
dominated environment, I was defensive – often without cause.
Over time and through experience, I began to realize that I needed
to get to know people before I assumed they were being critical of
me. Often, my perception of their view was not at all what I thought.
Try to stop yourself from making assumptions about what someone
else is thinking; often what we assume we hear is what we are telling
ourselves. I also used to judge work assignments by the person who
filled the role before me. Once I was very upset about a job I was
asked to do, solely based on the previous person who had the role.
In the end, I did the job my way, and it was really fun and fulfilling. It's
important to look at each opportunity in terms of what you can make
out of it. When I did that, I enjoyed everything.

Melissa Tata

Director Engineering Program Management, Dell Inc.

I would talk to myself as I was entering the workforce. I would encourage myself to be more vocal in meetings, even if I had to raise my hand to get attention. I would spend more time documenting and sharing my successes. I might take assignments that were closer tied to the customer so I could see my impact on society better. I would be more vocal in asking for what I wanted/deserved. Finally, I would understand the value of balance sooner – I often found that I accomplished the most based on long hours vs. providing impact based on my unique skills/knowledge. There have been many lessons I've learned via SWE and having a family, such as empathy, that would have made me a stronger leader earlier in my career; however, I spent my time in the office focused on delivering project results. Having a family earlier also would have provided me with a common conversation topic, which was sometimes a struggle with male counterparts since I have more typical female interests. I would also literally take a seat at the table. In executive reviews it is easier to contribute when you are seated beside those with influence.

Karen Tokashiki

Director, Northrop Grumman Corporation

When I was a young engineer, I never dreamed of the possibilities or extent of the goals that I could achieve. However, throughout my career, various managers and mentors opened my eyes to those possibilities, and I was able to achieve even higher leadership positions than I had ever imagined. Along the way, there were some lessons that I wish I had learned earlier:

Don't be afraid to ask for help – don't go it alone. Try new things and take more risks early on in your career, particularly if you are planning on starting a family, as it does get more difficult to balance. Grow technically, and take advantage of training and as many growth opportunities as your life balance allows you. Explore different paths, and don't be afraid to ask for new opportunities. Find out as much as you can about how your company operates, and the different career paths and opportunities available. Find out about and consider rotational opportunities. Talk with executives and management about their career paths. Get involved in employee network groups, or create a new group, if one doesn't exist at your company. Focus on building and maintaining mentoring relationships and peer networks. Think about long-range goals, and seek advice from trusted mentors. Think about what you want your legacy to be, and connect that with your brand.

Shirley Yap

GM Planning - Downstream Manufacturing, Shell Oil Company

The 4 Ps

As a young woman engineer, I learned that I must speak up and ask for what I want. At Shell I was given the freedom to express myself, and the support to grow and develop. Early in my career, I identified four principles that have been my guide to a successful career. I call them the 4 Ps - Passion, Personal Leadership, Prioritize, and Packaging.

1. **Passion:** Follow your passion. Listen to that voice in your heart.

2. **Personal Leadership:** Take the lead. Take control. In the long run, your leadership will be recognized.

3. **Prioritize:** When you are young, it is easy to "do it all." Instead, you must learn to prioritize. This is much harder than it sounds, but the long-term effect is huge. Say, "No." Keep balance. Do this early in your career, and you will benefit later.

4. **Packaging:** This refers to the total package that you present — personally and professionally. Have a crisp, clear story of what you want and what you are trying to say. Speak up. Make decisions and move on — be prepared to support your decisions. Show confidence.

Contributors' Bios

Decie Autin, Project Executive, ExxonMobil

In her current role as the Project Executive for the PNG LNG Project, Decie is responsible for planning, development, and execution of all aspects of the Project. Prior to this role, she held the position of Upstream Project Manager and was accountable for the engineering, procurement, and construction of the upstream portions of the PNG LNG Project, including the Hides Gas Conditioning Plant and 700km of pipeline to the LNG Plant.

Decie has been with ExxonMobil for over 30 years. She began her career in New Orleans in the offshore facilities surveillance team and moved within the organization in facilities and mechanical engineering management, natural gas and gas liquids marketing, Continuous Improvement Advisor, and Operations Superintendent. After 15 years in New Orleans, Decie moved to Houston into the Natural Gas Planning organization. Decie has been the Hoover-Diana Technical Manager and Startup Manager, the Thunder Horse OBO Interface Manager, and the Erha SURF Project Manager. Her most recent assignment prior to joining PNG LNG involved providing support for projects with significant sub-sea and pipeline engineering components.

Priyadarshini Bajoria, Group Manager (Client Services) and Associate Vice President, Infosys Ltd.

Priya D. Bajoria is a Group Manager (Client Services), Associate Vice President and Geo Cluster Head with Infosys Ltd. based in New York

City. Infosys (NYSE: INFY) is a global leader in consulting, technology and outsourcing solutions, with US $8.2B in annual revenues and 160,000+ employees. Priya manages a portfolio of clients in Infosys's Financial Services vertical and is one of the few women leaders in the Client Services organization. She has successfully steered and developed critical client relationships, which is testimony of her strong knowledge of the business environment and ability to structure technology enabled solutions to propel their businesses forward. In her capacity as Geo-Cluster Head for the New York and New Jersey areas, Priya spearheads a multi-pronged program for employee engagement and community outreach.

In the past, Priya has led the Consulting Practice in Capital Markets and has been credited with the successful delivery of complex engagements in the areas of investment banking, brokerage and customer service enablement. Prior to joining Infosys, she was an investment banker with Merrill Lynch in Mumbai where she executed several complex IPO and M&A transactions. Through her 20 year career spanning investment banking, consulting and client relationship management, Priya has worked across the U.S., UK and Asia, and is currently living in New York. Priya has earned an MBA degree in Finance and a Bachelor's degree in Computer Science from leading universities in India.

Liz Buzzard, R&D Scientist, The Clorox Company

Liz Buzzard is a Scientist in R&D Packaging Development at the Clorox Company in the Specialty Division. When Clorox develops or changes a product, she designs and tests primary and secondary packaging for compatibility with the new product or formula.

She manages all aspects of packaging- from conception to full scale production. She graduated from the University of Illinois at Urbana-Champaign in 2012 with a BS in Materials Science and Engineering and minors in the Hoeft Technology & Management Program and German. Her hobbies include hiking, running, reading, and of course, SWE. Liz has been involved with SWE since 2007, and is currently serving as a Region A Senator.

Marietta Cleveland, Quality Center Manager, Chrysler Group LLC

Marietta is currently the Quality Center Manager at Chrysler's Conner Avenue Assembly Plant where the Viper supercar is built. Prior to her tenure at Conner, she held the same position at the Warren Truck Assembly Plant where the Ram pick-up truck is built. In this role, she managed a department of 151 people of which, 12 were engineers, 14 were management, and 135 bargaining unit employees. Earlier in her career, Marietta worked in Product Engineering where she had responsibility for the Aero/Thermal Test Operations within the area of Scientific Labs. In this role, she managed a department of over 50 employees that performed vehicle climatic tests in order support the overall development and validation of vehicles. This included aerodynamics, thermal, wiper, and battery systems in real world conditions. In addition to the operations, she provided direction on vehicle instrumentation and test procedures to increase the overall efficiency of the process.

During her 28 year career with Chrysler, Marietta has held positions with increasing responsibility beginning as a Skilled Trades supervisor at Belvidere Assembly Plant. Later, she relocated to the Detroit area where she was promoted to Maintenance Area Manager at Warren Truck Assembly Plant. Notably, this position gave her the distinction of being the first African American Woman at Chrysler to hold this position. Throughout her career, Marietta has never been afraid of seeking new challenges and exploring endless opportunities. After 11 years in Manufacturing, Ms. Cleveland decided it was time to understand the engineering side of the business, and accepted a position in Product Engineering in the Scientific Laboratory & Proving Grounds organization where she held numerous positions.

Outside of work, Marietta is an active member of her church where she has served as the Women's Ministry Team lead and she also works with the church's Operations team.

Marietta has a Bachelor of Science in Electrical Engineering from the University of Michigan – Ann Arbor, MI and an MBA from Oakland University – Rochester Hills, MI.

Lisa Engel, Vice President New Product Development and Marketing, Emerson

Lisa Engel is the Vice President of Product Development and Marketing for ClosetMaid, an industry leader in home organization and storage systems. ClosetMaid is a business unit of Emerson Electric Co. She holds a BS in Engineering Mechanics and a MS in Mechanical Engineering. She launched her career working for aerospace manufacturers and defense contractors. After receiving her MBA, Lisa transitioned into a consumer marketing role at Wisconsin-based InSinkErator Company, another business unit of Emerson, guiding business growth platforms. Recently, she circled back to her roots in product development and engineering. Lisa currently resides in Florida, a long way and a few degrees warmer than Wisconsin, where she was born and raised. She has two active pre-teens who keep her thinking about home organization 24 hours a day. To see how ClosetMaid can help you get organized, visit closetmaid.com.

Diane Foley, Sr. Director, Mission Assurance, Raytheon

Diane Foley is a New York City native who was destined to be an engineer. She attended The Cooper Union for the Advancement of Science and Art, where she earned a Bachelor of Science in ttvMechanical Engineering. Diane went on to earn her Master of Business Administration while working full time. With a strong patriotic streak instilled in her by her father, she has worked her entire career in the defense industry, most recently as Sr. Director of Mission Assurance at Raytheon. Over the course of her career, Diane has held a number of different roles, from Acquisition Integration to business continuity management to vice president of Performance Excellence. Diane had her one and only son, Thomas, while she was in college. That's when she learned that even if you use a sing-song tone of voice when reading Advanced Thermodynamics, it is not a substitute for The Cat in the Hat. Over the course of her career, she has lived in NY, NJ, MD, MN, VA, and MA. Diane is still waiting for that elusive international assignment.

Gayle Gibson, Director of Engineering, DuPont

Gayle J. Gibson leads the DuPont Engineering Research and Technology organization of internal engineering consultants and the company's Field Engineering Program for early-career engineers. Gayle joined DuPont in 1983 and held a variety of roles through which she implemented best practices and enabled global business revitalization on behalf of multiple, high-performing business units. Her contributions included engineering design, process engineering, research and development, product and process development, manufacturing supervision, market development, business strategy, growth and supply chain improvement.

From 2008 -2013, Gayle was Director - Corporate Operations for the Chair of the Board of Directors and Chief Executive Officer of DuPont. In that role, she facilitated processes and engagement among key DuPont operating and leadership teams. This included working vacross businesses, functions, and regions to drive alignment and clarity on priorities, advancing core values, and resolving issues in line with the company's mission and strategic objectives. She also supported the Chief Executive Officer as co-lead of the National Academy of Engineering project "Changing the Conversation – from Research to Action" to improve the public understanding of engineering.

A certified Six Sigma Champion, Gayle holds a Bachelor of Science in chemical engineering from Texas A&M University and a Master of Business Administration from the European University. She is a member of AIChE, Tau Beta Pi, and the Society of Women Engineers.

Lynda Grindstaff, Director of Innovation Solutions, Intel Security Group, Intel Corporation

Lynda Grindstaff creates the future for Intel's Security Group as a Director of Innovation Solutions. Her tenure at Intel spans almost two decades and includes business client strategist, innovation marketing manager, client marketing engineer, system software development, chipset validation, and management of a global technical marketing team based in the US and India. As respected expert in her field, she has a patent and won the Intel Achievement Award, the Intel Software Quality Award, and the Society of Women Engineers Emerging Leader Award. A valued industry conference speaker, Lynda holds a BS in Computer Science from California State University Sacramento. She has a passion for coaching, growing, and developing technical leaders and remains active in community outreach programs for the Society of Women Engineers, National Center for Women & Information Technology, and the Women at Intel Network.

Rachel Heidenreich, Vice President of Quality and Continuous Improvement, Rockwell Automation

Rachel is Vice President of Quality and Continuous Improvement for Rockwell Automation, located in Mayfield Heights, OH. In this role, she manages engineers supporting field quality, quality assurance in the design of new products, supplier quality, and operations quality. She has worked for Rockwell for over five years. Prior to this role, Rachel worked for more than 20 years at GM and Delphi, an automotive supplier company. There, she served in a variety of engineering and business leadership roles that included a three-year assignment in Wuppertal, Germany. Rachel has a mechanical engineering degree from Penn State and an MBA from University of Virginia's Darden School of Business.

Afsaneh Sunnie House, Vice President, Southwest Coast Sub Region Manager, URS Corporation

Ms. House is a Vice President with the URS Corporation and serves as the Manager of the Southwest Coast Sub Region, which covers San Diego, Southern Nevada, Hawaii, and Guam Engineering and Construction Services. She also serves as the Operations Manager for the San Diego Office. She Joined URS in January 2006. As a registered civil engineer in California, she has managed and designed numerous complex transportation and public works projects in California and Hawaii for 30 years. She has also served as principal-in-charge for numerous design-build and design projects for highways, transit, and airport infrastructure. Featured in the book Changing Our World: True Stories of Women Engineers (Sybil E. Hatch, 2006), Ms. House has been a strong advocate for diversity in the workplace and, more specifically, for the role women can play in the leadership of organizations. She currently leads a global initiative for URS Infrastructure and Environment Division to develop and implement strategies to retain and recruit women. In November 2010, she was honored by the WTS Los Angeles Chapter as one of top 25 most influential women in the region's transportation industry.

Ms. House is a former President of WTS – an international organization, which focuses on advancing women in the transportation industry. In addition, she has served on the boards of several other professional organizations including: the Urban Land Institute (ULI), the California Transportation Foundation (CTF), California American Council of Engineering Companies (ACEC), and Greater San Diego Regional Chamber of Commerce Transportation Committee. Ms. House graduated from California State University Long Beach with a bachelor's degree in Civil Engineering in 1982.

Jennifer Howland, Executive, Pathways for Experienced Technical Women, IBM

Jennifer Howland is an engineer with her masters who has been working with IBM for 29 years. Jennifer leads IBM's Pathways Program, a worldwide program to develop bold actions to increase the representation of women in STEM-related leadership positions by recruiting and developing experienced mid-career technical women. Jennifer's work in IBM as an engineer, manager and executive has spanned engineering, strategy, development, transformation and services. Through her numerous management and executive level roles in male-dominated environments she has have always been passionate about helping women advance in their careers.

Stacy Johnson, Americas eMarketing Manager, Agilent Technologies

Stacy Kalisz Johnson is the Americas eMarketing Manager in the Field Marketing Organization at Agilent Technologies' Electronic Measurement Group, which is becoming Keysight Technologies. Stacy leads a team that specializes in using the power of the Internet as a business marketing tool, while accelerating lead capture for multiple sales channels. The programs from Stacy's team touch thousands of prospects and contacts per month, generating potential business. Hands on roles in application engineering, process engineering, and product marketing have provided great experience leading up to this role.

Stacy is a wife and mother of three boys and a dog. She enjoys playing soccer, spending time with her Zeta Tau Alpha sisters, and volunteering for the Go Red! for Women cause. Stacy started volunteering with Go Red! and the American Heart Association due to a family history of heart disease. In recent years, that passion has evolved to include fitness coaching with an alignment to Team Beachbody as an Independent Coach, helping people lead healthier and more fulfilling lives.

Stacy holds a BS and MS in mechanical engineering from the Rochester Institute of Technology and a Master Certificate in Project Management from George Washington University.

Dr. Ruth Jones, Mishap Investigation Specialist, NASA Safety Center

Dr. Ruth D. Jones is Mishap Investigation Specialist at the NASA Safety Center in Huntsville, Alabama. Dr. Jones performs extensive planning and preparatory work to ensure that mishap investigation teams are trained and available to support the rapid deployment of the Mishap Investigation Team and the effective and efficient conduct of Type A/Type B/High-Visibility Mishap Investigations.

Dr. Jones is an alumnus of Alabama A & M University, where she received her Doctorate of Philosophy and Masters of Science degrees in Physics/Materials Science in December 2000 and July 1997, respectively. She received her Bachelor of Science degree in Physics from the University of Arkansas in Pine Bluff in May, 1994. She was a 1989 honor graduate of Central High School, West Helena, Arkansas. Dr. Jones is the second African American woman to receive a PhD in Physics in the state of Alabama, and the first woman to receive a Bachelor of Science degree in Physics from the prestigious University of Arkansas at Pine Bluff.

Dr. Jones, the author of numerous articles on optical physics, is a member of the System Safety Society, Society of Women Engineers, American Physical Society, SPIE, and Delta Sigma Theta Sorority, Incorporated.

One of her goals is to help young people, particularly minorities in small towns, understand the excitement, opportunities, and enjoyment in pursuing a technical career.

A native of West Helena, Arkansas, Dr. Ruth Jones is the daughter of William and Essie Jones of West Helena, AR.

Andrea Karalus, Mechanical Design Discipline Chief, Pratt & Whitney

Andrea Karalus is a Mechanical Design Discipline Chief for Pratt & Whitney's Global Services Engineering Group. Her responsibilities for the aftermarket engineering business segment include: establishing training of the mechanical design practitioners; utilizing and creating tools to perform repair design assessment; and implementing processes to produce competitively superior mechanical solutions.

Andrea's career has spanned over 27 years at Pratt & Whitney, a division of United Technologies, initially working as an analytical engineer performing external aerodynamic analysis on engine inlets, exhaust nozzles, and engine installations. Her interest in mechanical design and manufacturing was fueled by early exposure to a design and fabrication services group that she worked with in order to manufacture a miniature wind tunnel.

Andrea earned her BS in mechanical engineering at the State University of New York at Buffalo and her MS in mechanical engineering from Rensselaer Polytechnic Institute. As a student, she became the president of the Engineering Student Association (ESA) at the university, sharing an office with the other officers of ESA, SWE, Tau Beta Pi, and the Professional Engineering Society.

A senior life member of the Society of Women Engineers, Andrea became a member as a sophomore and attended her first Society Conference in Washington, DC. Once she graduated and moved to Connecticut, she became active in the SWE Hartford Section, holding many leadership positions, including treasurer, vice-president, president, and section representative.

Andrea has been married for over twenty years and has two teenage children. She recently started taking piano lessons and has her pilot license.

Mariana Karam, Business Manager-Front End Equipment, Global Crop Harvesting Platform, John Deere

Mariana joined John Deere Harvester Works in 1991 as a Quality/Reliability Engineer. Since then, she has held leadership positions in Product Development, Supply Management, Manufacturing Engineering, Operations, Quality, and Service Parts. Her experience spans across multiple John Deere product lines and locations worldwide, including leadership of international supply management teams in China, India, Japan, and Korea, as well as expatriate assignments as Supply Management Manager at JD Brasil - Horizontina and as Factory Manager of the JD Fabriek Horst sprayer operations in the Netherlands. Most recently, Mariana served as Director, Enterprise Quality Services, where she led the development of the company's quality and business framework, the John Deere Quality and Production System. Currently, Mariana is responsible for executing Deere's Global Crop Harvesting front-end equipment strategy and programs for harvesting solutions worldwide. Prior to joining John Deere, Mariana served as a captain in the US Marine Corps.

Mariana is originally from Washington, DC. She's married to a fellow John Deere engineer, Jeff Hawkinson. Mariana holds BS and MS degrees in Mechanical Engineering from the University of Notre Dame and from Bradley University, respectively, as well as an MBA from Arizona State University.

Ellen Kerr, Vice President, Operations Engineering Manager, FM Global

Ellen Kerr graduated from Purdue University with a Bachelor of Science degree in Industrial Engineering. She started her career with Factory Mutual Engineering in their Chicago Office as a Loss Prevention Consultant.

Three years later, she joined Sara Lee Corporation in the Risk Management Department of their worldwide headquarters in Chicago. There, she served in the role of Property Conservation Engineer. In this capacity she conducted loss prevention inspections, drove risk improvement, and conducted plan reviews for Sara Lee facilities around the world.

She returned to the Factory Mutual System six years later as a Senior Account Engineer. In 2003, she joined the Los Angeles Office as a Group Manager of Field Engineers. In this role, she managed a group of 11 field engineers and was responsible for a book of business of $73.7m in total insurable value.

After four years, she decided to try the other coast, where she was Group Manager of Account Engineers in the Philadelphia Office. There, she managed a team of five account engineers and $102m in premiums.

The South then beckoned, and she became the Western Division Engineering Manager based in Plano, Texas. In this role, she oversaw the engineering processes, procedures, and people in five offices, including those in Sao Paulo, Brazil and Stockholm, Sweden. In her current role, Ellen is back in Chicago as the Operations Engineering Manager. She is directly responsible for the entire engineering staff comprising approximately 90 people and $324m in premium.

Ellen also serves as the engineering representative of FM Global on the Society of Women Engineers (SWE) Corporate Partnership Council, as well as being on the Qualifications Board for the Society of Fire Protection Engineers (SFPE).

Susan Lewis, Vice President, Dow AgroSciences Operations, The Dow Chemical Company

Susan Lewis is Vice President of Dow AgroSciences Operations. She is a member of the Dow Chemical (Dow) Operations Leadership Team and the Dow AgroSciences Corporate Management Committee. Lewis is responsible for all aspects of Dow AgroSciences' Manufacturing, Supply Chain, and Operational Environment, Health & Safety(EH&S).

Lewis joined Dow in manufacturing in 1987 and has held various manufacturing roles over her career. In addition to several Dow AgroSciences technologies, she has worked in emulsion polymers, cellulosics, monomers, polyglycols, and surfactants.

In 2008, she was named Dow AgroSciences Business Manufacturing leader (BML) for the Range and Pasture herbicides and Commodity insecticides business lines. Following the BML role, Lewis was named Dow AgroSciences Global Technology Center Director.

In May, 2010, Lewis was named Corporate Director of Dow EH&S Operations. Lewis served as Operations Director for Houston Operations, which includes the Deer Park, Lone Star, La Porte, and Bayport facilities from 2012 - 2014.

Lewis was a founding member of the Campbell Institute of the National Safety Council and is a member of the Society of Women Engineers. She serves on the industry board for Michigan Technological University (MTU) and was inducted into the Presidential Council of Alumnae for MTU. Lewis was named into the Distinguished Academy of Chemical Engineers, and in 2013 received the STEP award from the Manufacturing Institute. In 2014, she received the prestigious Next Generation Leadership award from the Manufacturing Leadership Council.

She is on the Board of Directors of Michigan 2-1-1 Health and Human Services Information and Referral, and is a Board member on the National Action Council for Minorities in Engineering (NACME). Lewis holds a bachelor's degree in chemical engineering from Michigan Tech University. She is based in Indianapolis, Indiana, at the global headquarters of Dow AgroSciences.

Nan Mattai, Senior Vice President, Engineering and Technology, Rockwell Collins

Nan Mattai is Senior Vice President of Rockwell Collins Engineering & Technology. Additionally, she is a corporate officer of Rockwell Collins. Ms. Mattai is responsible for Rockwell Collins' Engineering

& Technology organization, including the Advanced Technology Center. In this role, she is responsible for guiding the future technology direction, technology investment decisions, and the development of advanced technologies to meet the needs of the business portfolios. She was appointed to the position in November, 2004.

Previously, Ms. Mattai served as Vice President, Government Systems Engineering, a position to which she was appointed in 2001. She joined the company in 1993 and has held positions of increasing responsibility, including Senior Director of Tactical Communications, Government Systems.

Ms. Mattai is a member of: the Advisory Board, Aviation Week Strategic Media & Conferences; School of Systems & Enterprises, Stevens Institute of Technology; and the Iowa State University Institute for Physical Research and Technology (IPRT). Nan graduated from the University of Windsor, Canada with a Master's degree in nuclear physics and completed all graduate courses for a Doctorate in physics.

Maryann McNally, Vice President of the Innovation Center, ITW

Maryann McNally is Vice President of the Innovation Center at Illinois Tool Works Inc. (ITW). ITW is one of the world's leading diversified manufacturers of specialized industrial equipment, consumables, and related service businesses. ITW's products and solutions are at work all over the world, in deep-sea oil rigs, aerospace technology, bridges and wind turbines, healthcare, the spaces in which we live and work, the cars we drive, and the mobile devices we rely on. ITW (NYSE: ITW) is a Fortune 150 company that employs nearly 65,000 people, and is headquartered in Glenview, Illinois, USA, with operations in 58 countries.

Judy Moses, General Manager Asset Development, MidContinent Business Unit, Chevron

Judy Moses is the General Manager of Asset Development for Chevron's Mid-Continent business unit and has been in this position since June, 2010. She directs Chevron's upstream asset management and capital investment program in this business unit, which includes the regions from Texas, New Mexico, Oklahoma, and the Rockies. She has responsibility for a cross-functional organization that encompasses petroleum engineering, geosciences, and project management. She is presently transitioning to a similar position in Chevron's Southern Africa business unit in Luanda, Angola, with responsibility for major capital projects offshore Angola and the Republic of Congo.

Judy began her career with Texaco in 1988 as a petroleum engineer in Taft, California. She has held numerous upstream engineering and management positions with Texaco and Chevron in Texas, Louisiana, and California as well as Denmark, Indonesia, and Thailand.

Marla Peterson, Director, Engineering Operational Excellence, Honeywell Aerospace

Marla Peterson is the Director of Engineering &Technology Operational Excellence for Honeywell Aerospace. Operational Excellence's core functions are product development continuous improvement or productivity, project management, quality, and process maturity. Engineering Quality, Process Maturity, Learning, Productivity, and Advanced Methods comprise the department. Our purpose, ultimately, is to make the engineer as efficient as possible. Marla has worked at HON for over thirty years, and has been in leadership roles throughout her career. Marla began in the Mechanical area on analytical software for propulsion engines. She then devoted her attention to product data management for the capture of engineering knowledge. Marla is process focused and enables the use of her Lean Master and Black Belt experience with E&T to drive improvement and efficiencies.

Marla is a member of the Aero E&T Diversity Council. She represents Aero E&T at the Society of Women Engineering Conferences, serving as Booth Coordinator and HON SWE Awards Coordinator. She is a member of the Aerospace University Relations Council and serves as Campus Manager for the University of Arizona. She continues to mentor and sponsor interns and new hires. Each summer, Marla manages the E&T intern projects worked by intern groups throughout E&T.

Phoenix, Arizona is home for Marla, her husband Rob, and their boys, Max and Rex. Marla attended the University of Arizona where she received a degree in Systems Engineering. She is a HON Six Sigma Lean Master and Black Belt. She is a member of SWE, Tau Beta Pi, and the University of Arizona Alumni Organization.

Emily Plunkett, Senior Structural Engineer 3A, L-3 Mission Integration

From a young age, Emily always had an interest in science and mathematics. As a teenager, she became fascinated by aircraft, which lead her to pursue an Aerospace Engineering degree from Georgia Tech. After graduating from Georgia Tech in 2005, Emily took a job as a structural analyst at L-3 Communications, Mission Integration Division, analyzing structural modifications on aircraft. Since beginning there, she has worked on many different aircraft during various program stages, from preliminary proposals to aircraft integration.

Sharon Rozzi, Senior Director Operations, Medtronic

Sharon Rozzi is Senior Director Continuous Improvement at Medtronic. In this role, she is responsible for driving lean methodologies and culture in the Spinal business unit to ensure year over year improvement in product quality, delivery, and cost. She has nineteen years of experience as a medical device industry leader in Operations, R&D, and Program Management. She has been awarded fifteen US patents.

Sharon received her PhD in chemical engineering from Carnegie Mellon, and her Bachelor of Science degree in the same from Cornell. She also holds an MBA from the Carlson School of Management at the University of Minnesota.

Jennifer Rumsey, Vice President of Engineering, Engine Business, Cummins

Jennifer Rumsey is currently the Vice President of Engineering in the Engine Business at Cummins. In this role, she is responsible for new product development and product support globally for Cummins 2 - 15 liter engines, which serve a variety of on and off highway market applications. Her early career focused on control systems and system engineering, initially at a fuel processing and fuel cell start-up company in Cambridge, Massachusetts. In 2000, she moved to Cummins and has worked in a variety of engineering roles across Cummins' business units, including advanced technology development, new product development, and current product engineering.

Jennifer is a member of the Society of Women Engineers, Society of Automotive Engineers, and Women in Trucking Association. She holds a BSME from Purdue University and a MSME from Massachusetts Institute of Technology. Jennifer and her husband, Jim, have two daughters.

Vicky Saye, Vice President, Core Technology & Cost Optimization, Kellogg Company

Vicky Saye serves as Vice President of Core Technology and Cost Optimization and Sensory and Analytical Science. Her team partners with Global Supply Chain and the Business Units to execute network programs, quality improvements, and design to value initiatives. Her team is also accountable for the delivery of global sensory, chemistry, and statistics programs and processes. She provides leadership for the RQT Knowledge Management Program and is a member of the company's Research, Quality and Technology Leadership Team. Ms. Saye began her career at Kellogg in 1986 as an Engineer in Corporate Technology. She held various roles of increasing responsibility within the Engineering organization before moving to Research, Quality and Technology as part of the Launch Program Management team, where she led multiple initiatives for the North American and Latin American businesses.

Ms. Saye was promoted to Director, Operations, for the W.K. Kellogg Institute for Food & Nutrition Research in 2003, and Sr. Director, R&D, in 2004. She was promoted to Vice President, Core Technology and Cost Optimization in 2008, and promoted to her current role in 2012.

She received her BS and MS degrees in Agricultural Engineering from The Ohio State University, and she is a licensed professional engineer.
Ms. Saye and her husband, Tim, reside in the Battle Creek, Michigan area. They have two children.

Margaret Simone, Senior Project Manager, Turner Construction Company

Margaret Simone is a Senior Project Manager for Turner Construction Company. She is currently working on the Fort Lauderdale-Hollywood International Airport as a Senior Project Manager for the Terminal 4 Expansion project. Margaret has worked in several Turner offices across the country, including New York City, Nashville, Los Angeles, Atlanta, and Orlando. Projects include the Duval County Courthouse, University of North Florida Library, Vanderbilt Hospital's Medical Research Building, and several projects with the New York Interiors group. Margaret has a BS in Civil Engineering from Vanderbilt University.

Patricia Solliday, Senior R&D Engineer, Boston Scientific

Trish Solliday was born and raised in Saginaw, Michigan. She proceeded to a small state college in Baltimore, Maryland for two years, where she received an academic scholarship to study engineering. After declaring chemical engineering, she transferred to Hampton University in Virginia where, in her junior year, she received a National Consortium for Graduate Degrees for Minorities in Engineering and Science Scholarship, which set the stage for graduate school opportunities. Before graduating with her BS in Chemical Engineering, she completed two internships at Dow Chemical in Michigan.

Today, Trish is an established Senior R&D Engineer for Boston Scientific. She currently holds two primary responsibilities: support the design integrity of medical devices and strategically develop Product Lifecycle Process Value Improvements for BSC's Engineering

Services Group. The latter of these allows BSC to achieve multi-million dollar improvement goals annually.

Trish and her Husband Scott live in Inver Grove Heights, Minnesota, where they raise their three children and run their own business. She is active in the community, continuing to educate the youth on STEM opportunities. She holds a board member position for the YMCA Twin Cities and is passionate about diversity. Trish is attending the MBA evening program at the University of St. Thomas.

Lauren Streb, Tech Transfer Lead, Genentech

Lauren Streb leads tech transfer projects at Genentech, where she started her career in Biotech 11 years ago. She has held roles in Supply Chain, Manufacturing, and Project Management. In these positions, she supported the development, commercialization, and commercial supply of Drug Substance (API), Drug Product, and Finished Goods. She is a PMP and APICS CPIM and has a degree in Molecular and Cell Biology from UC Berkeley.

Jean Sweeney, Vice President, 3M

Jean Sweeney is Vice President for Environment, Health, Safety, and Sustainability Operations at 3M. With degrees in chemical engineering and business management, Ms. Sweeney has held a variety of positions with 3M, including product development, manufacturing management, general manager, and two international assignments as Manufacturing Director for 3M Australia in Sydney and Managing Director of 3M Taiwan in Taipei. In her current position, Ms. Sweeney is responsible for 3M's global environmental, health, and safety programs for 90,000 employees and 225 manufacturing locations worldwide. This includes technical and regulatory expertise in environmental management, safety, ergonomics, and industrial hygiene. In addition, Ms. Sweeney leads 3M sustainability strategy development and implementation for footprint reduction in global operations.

Melissa Tata, Director Engineering Program Management, Dell Inc.

Melissa Tata applies her mechanical engineering background and outstanding interpersonal skills to oversee execution of operations programs to reduce cost, augment customer experience, and improve cycle time. During her 14-year tenure at Dell, Melissa and the teams she led successfully drove more than $55 million in annual savings and optimal usage of more than $15 million in annual operating expense budgets. Melissa drove a Six Sigma Black Belt program to optimize manufacturing utilization by distributing orders based on delivery location. As an engineering director, she led partner alliance agreements and governance processes for a $26B business, and enhanced product profitability.

Melissa developed empowerment, strategic planning, and communication skills via leadership in the Society of Women Engineers (SWE) for which she served as Society President from 2011 to 2012. During her tenure, she participated in several White House events to promote recruitment and retention of girls and women in science, technology, engineering, and mathematics fields.
Melissa has a passion for manufacturing engineering and developing talent, and shares her experiences to encourage others. When she is not working, Melissa enjoys swimming, spending time with her son

and daughter, and participating in events with her alma maters MIT and Rensselaer Polytechnic Institute.

Karen Tokashiki, Director, Northrop Grumman Corporation

As director for Integration Competitive Analysis and Materials (ICAM), Karen Tokashiki is responsible for leading the 900-person functional homeroom that delivers technical support services across the traditional engineering disciplines.

Karen previously served as Director of Aerospace Engineering Technical Operations. She stood up this new organization focused on driving common strategy and integration across the newly consolidated engineering homeroom. In this position, Karen stood up the Aerospace Systems Women in Leadership program, which is now in its third year.

Karen joined Northrop Grumman in 1984, and has held many technical and management positions of increasing responsibility associated with the development, delivery, and operation of space-based ground and test systems. She received her Bachelor's degree in Electrical Engineering from University of California Davis and her Master's degree in Electrical Engineering from the Massachusetts Institute of Technology. She is a graduate of the UCLA Executive Management program and the Women Unlimited LEAD program. Karen has also completed the Corporate and Sector Leading1NG programs and the Program Management Conference.

Karen resides in Manhattan Beach. She enjoys snow and water skiing, musical activities, attending local sports games, and vacationing with her family.

Shirley Yap, General Manager of Planning for Downstream Manufacturing, Shell Oil Company

Shirley Yap is the General Manager of Planning for Downstream Manufacturing at Shell, overseeing the startup of US Fuels GSAP for Manufacturing Hydrocarbon Management.

Shirley joined Shell in 1995, and has broad experience across Manufacturing, and Supply and Distribution, from strategy to operational level, as well as business/commercial to asset management level. No matter the role, Shirley continually delivers record performance with global impact. She is a leader in driving change and improvements, and a strong supporter of talent development. As an advocate for Diversity and Inclusion, Shirley serves on the Executive Advisory Board for SAPENG; and also the Board of Directors for the Society of Asian Scientists and Engineers (SASE).

Shirley served as Unit Manager for Manufacturing Production from 2001-2006, and as a Portfolio Advisor for Manufacturing Strategy from 2006-2009. Her most recent roles were in Supply and Distribution; as General Manager of Global HSSE from 2010-2011; and North American Planning Manager for Refining Margin Optimization from 2011-2013.

Shirley holds a Bachelor of Science in Chemical Engineering from UCLA, and a Master of Science in Chemical Engineering from Northwestern University. In her spare time, Shirley enjoys travel, film, and activities with close friends and family.

59087351R00084

Made in the USA
San Bernardino, CA
02 December 2017